——— The Dictionary of ———
ACUPUNCTURE & MOXIBUSTION
An instant guide to the common and not so common
terminology used in acupuncture and moxibustion.

The Dictionary of
ACUPUNCTURE
& MOXIBUSTION

A Practical Guide to Traditional Chinese Medicine

Compiled and written by
Nguyen Duc Hiep
M.D., D.T.P.H., D.C.H., O.M.B.Ac.A.

THORSONS PUBLISHING GROUP
Wellingborough, Northamptonshire
———— · ————
Rochester, Vermont

Published in the UK by Thorsons Publishers Ltd.,
Denington Estate, Wellingborough, Northamptonshire NN8 2RQ,
and in the USA by Thorsons Publishers Inc.,
Park Street, Rochester, Vermont.

First published 1987

British Library Cataloguing in Publication Data

Nguyen, D. Hiep
    The dictionary of acupuncture and
    moxibustion: a practical guide to
    traditional Chinese medicine.
    1. Acupuncture — Dictionaries
    I. Title
    615.8'92'0321   RM184

    ISBN 0-7225-1290-2

Printed and bound in Great Britain

DEDICATION

To Anh, Chau, Quan.

ACKNOWLEDGEMENTS

I wish to express my thanks to the following individuals and institutions for permission to reproduce their photographs and drawings:

Dr F. Mann and William Heinemann Medical Books Ltd.
(Figure 28)

Mayfair Trading Company, Hong Kong
(Figures 22, 26, 31, 41, 42)

University of Hong Kong Libraries
(Figure 36)

D. Henrioud (WHO)
(Figure 54)

INTRODUCTION

Acupuncture has grown in popularity and importance in Europe only in the last thirty years, although it has been known in the West since the seventeenth century. In North America, acupuncture became popular only after the reopening of relations between America and China in 1972.

However, this development of acupuncture in the West is still slow and limited for two main reasons:

1. The language barrier. Chinese is not an easy language to translate, even if the original is perfectly understood and it is sometimes very difficult to explain Chinese medical concepts due to the relative lack of adequate equivalents in Western languages.

2. Great conceptual differences between Chinese and Western medicine. Chinese medicine has been in existence for over two millennia, well before the birth of modern medicine, and is founded on a philosophy, Taoist thinking and *Yin Yang* theory which are totally foreign to the West.

In recent years, a number of Chinese medical books and journals have been translated into Western languages, mostly French and English, and an increasing number of books, dealing particularly with acupuncture, written by Western authors, have been published. Readers who are not familiar with Chinese medicine, may be confused not only by the new medical concepts but also by the strange terminology. Moreover, Chinese terms are sometimes translated and interpreted differently according to the authors.

I have tried to select a number of terms commonly used in acupuncture as well as some Chinese medical terms which are more or less related to acupuncture and moxibustion to make this book a practical guide so that readers may quickly obtain a reasonable but concise amount of information about acupuncture and moxibustion. If they then require further information, they should refer to other books dealing with the subjects in detail.

The Chinese characters are given in addition to romanized and translated terms since the Chinese words can often be romanized and translated in many different ways and the pronunciation of many Chinese characters is identical while the meanings are quite different. The Vietnamese pronunciation is also included.

I hope that this book will be useful to acupuncturists and laymen for a better understanding of Traditional Chinese Medicine in general and acupuncture and moxibustion in particular.

A

abdomen, abdominal cavity [*Fu* 腹 *Phúc*], is the largest cavity in the body, extending from the diaphragm to the pelvis and is divided into: abdomen major (*Da fu*), located below the diaphragm and above the umbilicus, and abdomen minor (*Xiao fu*), located below the umbilicus.

absolute *Yin* syndrome [*Jueyin bing* 厥阴病 *Quyết Âm bệnh*], relates to the liver. The main characteristic of the syndrome is a prolonged course with alternate chills and fever. (see **diagnosis based on six channels**).

accumulation (*Xi*-cleft) points [*Xi xue* 郄穴 *Khích huyệt*], so called since these points are considered gaps or clefts (*Xi*) where the *Qi* of the channels converges and accumulates. There are sixteen accumulation points: twelve on the regular channels and four on the extra channels (Table 1). They are effective in acute disorders occuring in the areas supplied by their respective channels and those occuring in their respective related organs. For example, the points St34 and Lu6 are effective in epigastric pain and hemoptysis respectively.

activities of *Qi* [*Qi hua* 气化 *Khí hoá*], includes the vital function of the viscera, the circulation and distribution of *Qi* and **blood** etc.; and the regulation of water distribution of the **three heater.**

Table 1: The Accumulating (*Xi*-cleft) Points

REGULAR CHANNELS	ACCUMULATING POINTS
Lung	Lu6 (*Kongzui*)
Pericardium	P4 (*Ximen*)
Heart	H6 (*Yinxi*)
Large intestine	LI7 (*Wenliu*)
Three heater	TH7 (*Huizong*)
Small intestine	SI6 (*Yanglao*)
Stomach	St34 (*Liangqiu*)
Gall bladder	GB36 (*Waiqiu*)
Urinary bladder	UB63 (*Jinmen*)
Spleen	Sp8 (*Diji*)
Liver	Liv6 (*Foot-Zhongdu*)
Kidney	K5 (*Shuiquan*)
EXTRA CHANNELS	
Yang heel (*Qiao*)	UB59 (*Fuyang*)
Yin heel (*Qiao*)	K8 (*Jiaoxin*)
Yang tie (*Wei*)	GB35 (*Yangjiao*)
Yin tie (*Wei*)	K9 (*Zhubin*)

acupressure, see **finger puncture.**

acupuncture [*Zhen jiu* 針 灸 *Châm cúʾu*], is a method of inserting special needles into certain points on the body to treat disease and alleviate pain or to produce analgesia. This ancient Chinese art has been applied as a therapeutic medical technique in China for at least 2000 years. The term acupuncture, invented by Willem Ten Rhyne, a Dutch physician, after his journey to Japan in the seventeenth century, literally means to puncture with the needle (L. acus: needle; punctura: puncture). The Chinese term *Zhen Jiu* means acupuncture moxibustion and is more rational since, from ancient times, these two methods have often been used in co-ordination.

Acupuncture Questions and Answers [*Zhen jiu wen da* 針 灸 问 答 *Châm cúʾu vấń dáp*], this **catechism of acupuncture and moxibustion**

ACUPUNCTURE & MOXIBUSTION

was written by Wang Ji (AD 1463-1539) and published in AD 1530 in which the essential theories and principles of acupuncture and moxibustion are clearly explained in detail.

---

adverse *Qi* [*Ni Qi* 逆气 *Nghịch khí*], flows opposite to the normal direction. For example, nausea and vomiting caused by the stomach *Qi* that runs upward instead of the normal downward.

Ah shi **(ah yes) points** [*Ah shi xue* 阿是穴 *A thị huyệt*], are so called since the patient says this when the physician presses his finger on the right spot causing pain. These tender or sensitive spots are present in certain diseases and have neither definite locations nor special names. 'Puncture

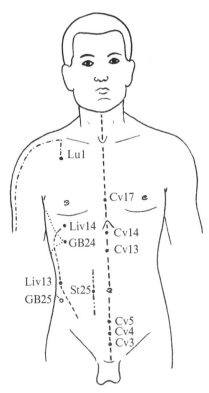

Fig. 1:   Alarm (front-*Mu*) points

13

wherever there is tenderness', (Sun Si-miao).

---

alarm (front -*Mu*) points [*Mu xue* 募穴 *Mộ huyệt*],   are where the *Qi* of the respective internal organs is infused and they are located on the chest and abdomen, close to their respective related organs (Fig. 1; Table 5). When a related organ is affected, an abnormal reaction such as tenderness may occur in the corresponding point. These alarm points are important in both diagnosis and treatment.

---

analgesia, acupuncture [*Zhen ci zhen tong* 针刺镇痛 *Châm thích trân thông*],   is a new method developed recently (1959) in China based on relieving pain by needling. It is the combination of traditional Chinese and Western medicine. Both terms acupuncture analgesia and acupuncture anaesthesia are freely used but the term acupuncture analgesia is more correct since the procedure results only in an absence of pain, the other senses remain unaffected. One or more needles are inserted into certain selected points on the limbs, ears, nose or face. Analgesia follows after a period of inducement and stimulation. Operations should be performed in less than an hour to avoid the phenomenon of tolerance. Patients are fully conscious during operations. Apart from being dulled or not sensitive to pain, they are normal in other physiological functions. The success rate varies; it is around 90 per cent according to the Chinese. A recent theory suggests that the insertion of needles may stimulate the release of a morphine-like substance which is produced naturally within the central nervous system and many other parts of the body and is called endorphins.

---

ancestral *Qi* [*Zong Qi* 宗气 *Tôn khí, tông khí*],   formed by the **clean** *Qi* from the atmosphere and the **grain** *Qi* from the essence of food, is stored in the chest. Its main function is to nourish the heart and the lungs and to promote their functions.

---

animal spirit [*Po* 魄 *Phách*],   is used to explain the Chinese term '*Po*' which has no equivalent in English. '*Hun*' or **soul** is of a high spiritual nature. It is one of the five spiritual resources and is controlled by the lungs. When someone is said to have plenty of *Po* or *Qi* and *Po*, it means that she or he is exceptionally brave and could tackle any confrontation. *Hun* and *Po* vanish when one is frightened to death. The acupuncture point UB42 *Pohu* (animal spirit house) is indicated in lung diseases. The Chinese terms *Pohan* and *Pomen* mean **sweat** and **anus** respectively.

---

anus [*Gang men* 肛 门 *Giang môn*],   another name for *Pomen* or animal spirit gate since it is through this gate that the end product of the lung air (*Fei Qi*) is evacuated.

---

apoplexy [*Zhong feng* 中风 *Trúng phong*],   literally, the Chinese term means being hit by the **evil wind**. Apoplexy or windstroke can be caused by: exogenous factor, stirring wind arising from hyperactivity of the liver *Yang* resulting from exasperation or agitation; and endogenous factor, caused by **phlegm-heat** after over-indulgence in alcohol and fatty diet. There are two types of apoplexy: severe, when the internal organs are attacked and the signs and symptoms are those of the collaterals, channels and internal organs; and mild, when only the **channels** and **collaterals** are attacked and the symptoms and signs are connected with the channels and collaterals.

---

appendicitis [*Lan wei yan* 阑 尾 炎 *Lan vĩ viêm*],   according to traditional Chinese medicine, is caused by: accumulation of **damp-heat** due to retention of food in the intestine; and stagnation of *Qi* and **blood** due to exposure to excessive **heat** or **cold**. The empirical extraordinary acupuncture point *Lanwei* is indicated in acute appendicitis.

Artimesia vulgaris [*Ai* 艾 *Ngài*],   *N.O. Compositae*: other names: mugwort, Felon herb, St John's herb — ancient magical plant once called 'mother of herbs' (Mater Herbarum) revered throughout Europe and Asia. The common name mugwort derives from the Old Saxon 'muggia wort' which means midge plant since it can repel the insects.

Description: an erect pubescent perennial growing three to four feet high with dark green pinnate or bipinnate leaves with toothed leaflets. The flowers are yellowish brown, appear from late summer to mid-autumn (Fig. 2).

Habitat: in waste land, hedgerows, near rivers and streams in Europe and Asia.

Cultivation: wild and cultivated. Grows quickly.

Constituents: volatile oil, resin, absinthin, a bitter principle which stimulates digestion.

Uses: formerly used for flavouring and clarification of beer; stuffing geese, ducks; as a diuretic, emmenagogue, stimulation of appetite, remedy for intestinal worms; fly and moth repellent; **moxibustion** in traditional Chinese medicine.

Fig. 2: *Artemisia vulgaris*

ashy and black fur [*Hui hei tai* 灰黑苔 *Khôi hăć dài*], in cases of endogenous **cold** or **cold and damp**, the tongue is usually pale with moistened, ashy black fur. Intense **heat** with impairment of *Qi* is manifested by a red dry tongue with ashy black fur.

---

associated (back-*Shu*) points [*Bei shu xue* 背 俞 穴 *Bôí du huyệt*], are points where the *Qi* of the respective internal organs is infused. These points are arranged on the back at either side of the vertebral column, in

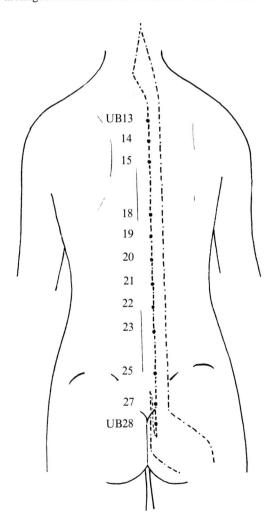

Fig. 3: Associated (back-*Shu*) points

close proximity to their respective related internal organs. The points become tender when the related organs are affected. All **channels** have an associated point (Table 5; Fig. 3) which plays an important part in the diagnosis and treatment of diseases involving their respective internal organs. The associated points can be used separately or in combination with the **alarm (front-*Mu*) points.**

---

asthma [*Shi chuan* 实 喘 *Thực suyễn*], is caused by excessive pathogenic factors in the **lungs** and characterized by rapid short breaths with profuse sputum. There are two types of asthma: excess (*Shi*) resulting from a dysfunction of the lungs in descending due to invasion of exogenous **wind cold** or disturbance of **phlegm heat;** and deficiency (*Xu*) when the **kidney** is deficient and cannot receive *Qi* (air).

B

---

back-*Shu* points,   see **associated points.**

---

bending of the needle [*Wan zhen* 弯 针 *Loan châm*],   an accident in acupuncture, generally happening when the needle is inserted with uneven finger pressure or too forcefully or when the needle strikes hard tissue.

Bi **syndrome** [*Bi* 痹 *Tê*],   pain and numbness caused by obstruction of the circulation of *Qi* and blood usually due to invasion of the **channels and collaterals** by **wind cold** and **damp** when the defensive *Qi* is weak. Arthralgia is the main feature. Swelling and joint deformities occur in chronic cases. Four main types of *Bi* syndrome are described:
1. *wandering Bi:* or migratory arthralgia;
2. *painful Bi:* arthralgia responds to warmth and is aggravated by cold;
3. *fixed Bi:* fixed arthralgia;
4. *febrile Bi:* tenderness, swelling, redness of the affected joints. One or several joints may be affected at the same time.

Bi **syndromes, five** [*Wu bi* 五痺 *Ngũ tê*], refer to the five pain and numbness syndromes of the skin, flesh, muscles, bones and pulse which are caused by **eight winds.**

Bian Que [扁鵲 *Biêu' Thố'c*], was, according to Szuma Chien's *Historical Records* (*Shi Ji*), the earliest famous physician who lived in the state of Zheng during the Warring States period (475-221 BC). It is commonly believed that Bian Que was Qin Yue-ren, author of the *Difficult Classic* (*Nan Jing*). He was renowned for his talent in medicine particularly in diagnosis and treatment and was ascribed the authorship of some medical books such as *The Internal Classic of Bian Que* (*Bian Que Nei Jing*) and *The External Classic of Bian Que* (*Bian Que Wai Jing*). His method of diagnosis, still in use today, consists of four main points:

1. noting the patient's spirit, facial colour, posture, tongue coating;
2. listening to the body sounds and smelling the body odours;
3. enquiring about headache, pain, appetite etc.;
4. palpation, i.e. feeling the pulse and pressing the affecting points or parts of the body.

big pulse [*Da mai* 大脈 *Dại mạch*], the wave amplitude is double of that of the normal pulse. The big pulse can be either strong (in case of excessive **evil heat** and normal body resistance) or weak (in case of general debility).

bile [*Dan zhi* 胆汁 *Dảm trấp*], is an important aid to the digestion of foods and fluids, and is excreted by the **gall bladder.** If its production is disrupted, symptoms such as jaundice, bitter taste in the mouth, nausea, vomiting, and distension of the flanks will occur. It is believed that bile has a strong influence on the spirit or character of people. The Chinese term *Dan Da* (great gall bladder or plenty of bile) means bold, audacious. *Dan Xiao* (small gall bladder or scanty bile) means timid, cowardly.

Bin Hu's *Pulse Studies* [*Bin Hu mai xue* 濒湖脈学 *Tân Hồ mạch học*], written by Li Shi-zhen, *hao*-name Bin-hu (AD 1518-1593) in 1564, describes in detail 27 kinds of pulse and their diagnostic value.

blood [*Xue* 血 *Huyết*], in traditional Chinese medicine, is not the same as that of the Western medicine. Blood, regarded as a *Yin* substance, is formed from the essence of food, the body fluid and the essence of the **kidney** (kidney *Jing*). Blood and *Qi* are closely related: the formation and circulation of blood depend upon *Qi* while the production and distribution of *Qi* are controlled by blood. 'Although different in name, blood and *Qi* are of the same class.'

---

blood chamber [*Xue shi* 血室 *Huyết thất*], a term referring to: the **uterus**, the **liver**, the **penetrating (Chong) channel.**

---

boiling pulse [*Fu fei mai* 釜沸脉 *Phủ phị mạch*], an extremely floating and rapid pulse, one of the seven pulses indicating impending death.

---

bone [*Gu* 骨 *Cốt*], one of the six curious or **extraordinary organs** mentioned in ancient literature. Since the bones contain medulla (*Sui*) which is manufactured by the **kidneys,** in cases of bone diseases, the kidneys or the kidney channel should be investigated and treated. 'The bones are nourished by the marrow and ruled by the kidneys.'

---

bone measurement [*Gu du* 骨度 *Cốt độ*], a proportional measurement of the human body for locating acupuncture points according to the length and size of a given bone of the individual (see **inch**).

Book of Changes [*Yi jing* 易经 *Dịch kinh*], one of the five *Classics of Confucianism* (*Wu Jing*), used for divination, it is a series of brief texts for a sequence of sixty-four symbolic hexagrams which, if properly interpreted, are said to contain profound meanings (see **eight trigrams**). The four other Classics are: *Book of Songs, Book of History, Book of Rites, Spring-Autumn Annals.*

---

brain [*Nao* 脑 *Não*], one of the six curious or **extraordinary organs** mentioned in classical literature, its main functions are thinking and memorization. It is the source of *Jing* or essence of life. As described in

Nei Jing 'the brain is the sea of marrow' and since the marrow that forms the brain is produced by the **kidney,** in case of diseases related to the brain, the function of the kidney should be investigated.

broken needle [*Duan zhen* 断针 *Doạn châm*], an accident in acupuncture which may be due to: forceful manipulation; muscular spasm; changing of position of the patient; needle of poor quality; needle with eroded base. Surgery is needed if the needle breaks under the skin.

C

Canon of Medicine, see **Nei Jing.**

cardia [*Ben men* 贲门 *Bôn môn*], one of the seven passes along the alimentary tract (see **seven passes**).

catechism of acupuncture and moxibustion, see *Acupuncture Questions and Answers.*

catgut embedding therapy [*Mai xian liao fa* 埋线疗法 *Mai tuyên liệu pháp*], a piece of catgut is embedded in a selected point to produce protracted stimulation.

cauterization [*Shao zhuo* 烧灼 *Thiêu chu'ó'c*], also called scarring moxibustion, involves placing a small cone on the selected point and burning. This method is indicated in certain chronic diseases such as **asthma,** but has been discredited since it is painful and leaves unsightly scars.

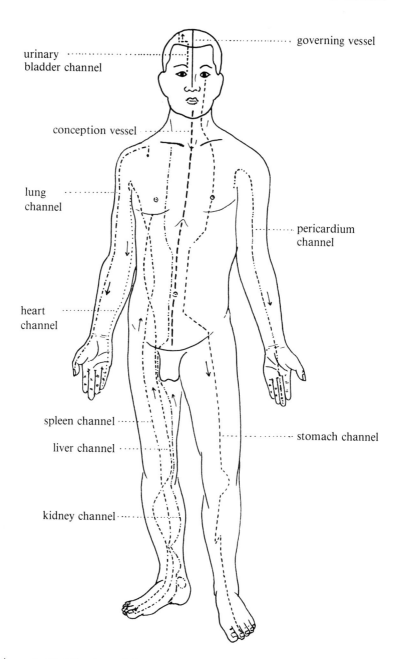

Figure 4: Distribution of fourteen channels (anterior view)

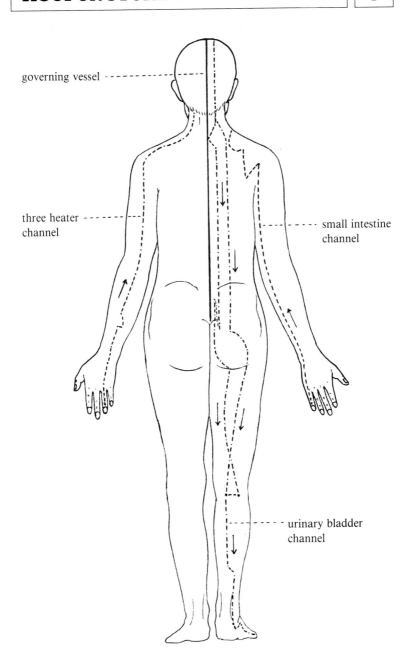

Figure 5: Distribution of fourteen channels (posterior view)

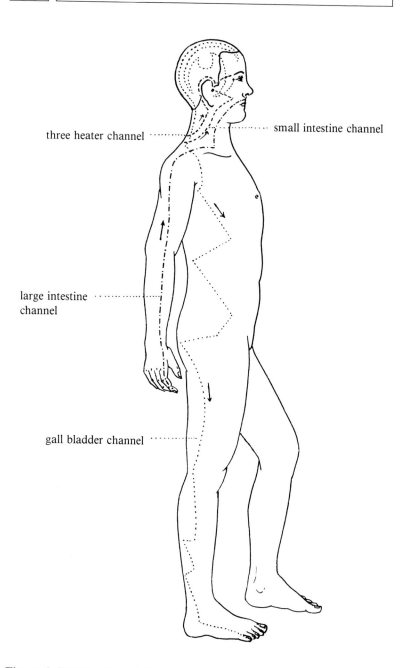

three heater channel

small intestine channel

large intestine channel

gall bladder channel

Figure 6: Distribution of fourteen channels (lateral view)

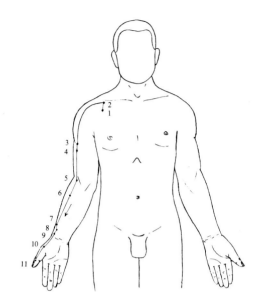

Figure 7: The lung channel of hand-*Taiyin*

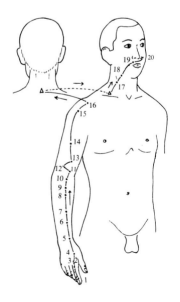

Figure 8: The large intestine channel of hand-*Yangming*

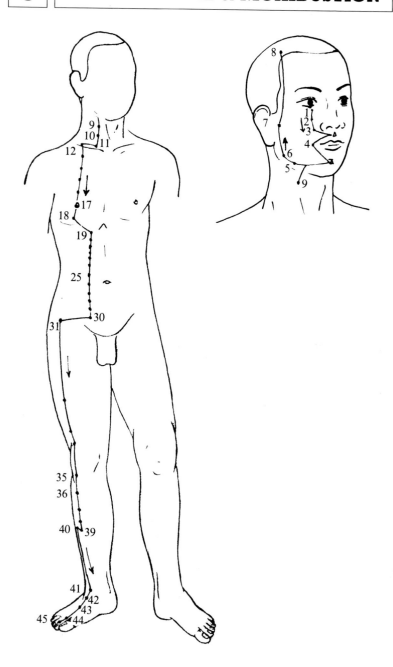

Figure 9: The stomach channel of foot-*Yangming*

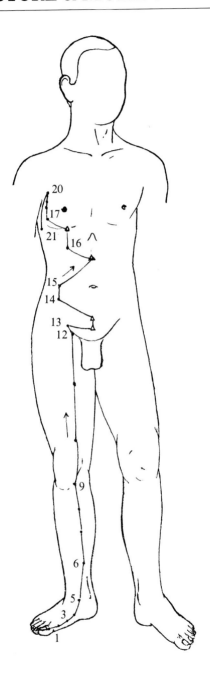

Figure 10: The spleen channel of foot-*Taiyin*

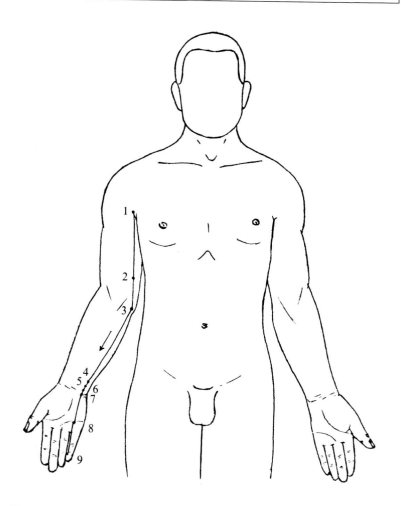

Figure 11: The heart channel of hand-*Shaoyin*

channels and collaterals [*Jing luo* 经络 *Mai luo* 脉络 *Kinh lộ, mạch lộ (lạc)*], '*Jing*' means to go through, vessel, vein or artery, meridian of longitude and can be translated either as meridian after the French translation or as channel. The term channel is however a better translation than meridian since it gives the impression of a three dimensional conduit. It is just an imaginary line linking a certain number of points on the body surface which have the same therapeutic and diagnostic properties on a definite organ. '*Mai*' means conduit, vessel, pulse; '*Luo*' refers to something resembling a net.

Channels are of two types:

1. main or regular channels (*Jing mai* or *Jing*) are those which run longitudinally or transversally;

2. collaterals (*Luo mai* or *Luo*), are smaller and emerge from the main channels.

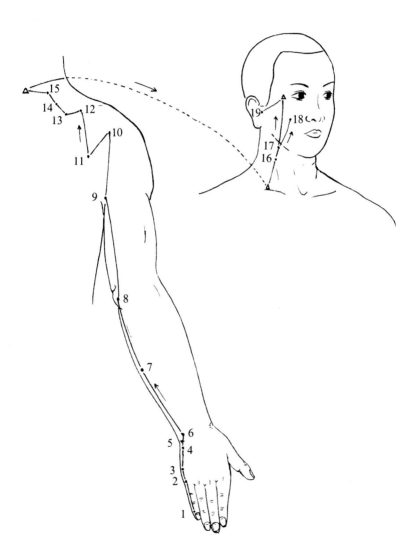

Figure 12: The small intestine channel of hand-*Taiyang*

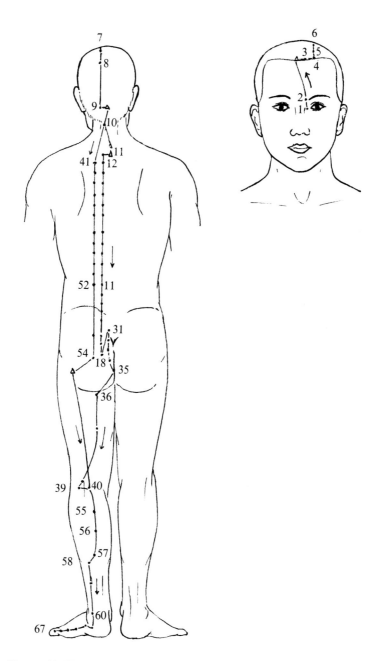

Figure 13: The urinary bladder channel of foot-*Taiyang*

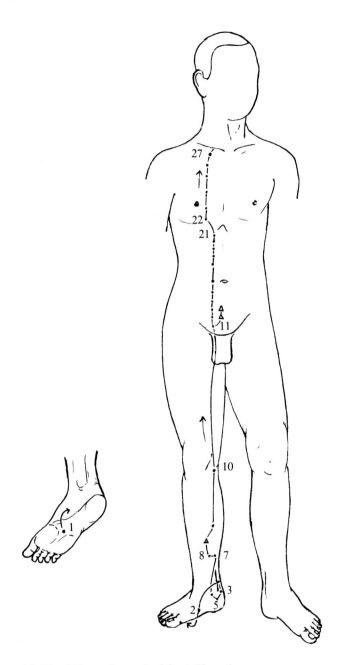

Figure 14: The kidney channel of foot-*Shaoyin*

There are in total fourteen main channels formed by twelve channels pertaining to twelve **internal organs** and two (**governing** and **conception** vessels) of the eight extra channels (Figs. 4-18). Each of the main channels has its own system of collaterals. There are fifteen collaterals including

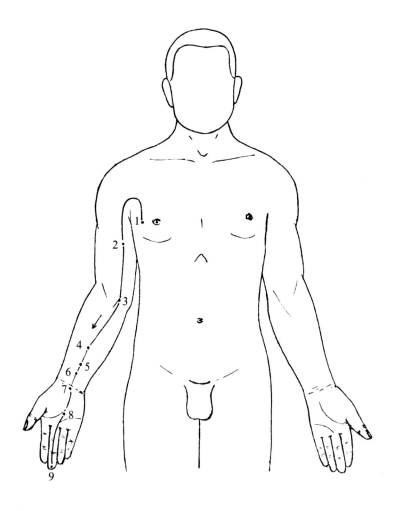

Figure 15: The pericardium channel of hand-*Jueyin*

the major collateral of the **spleen.** The channels are named after the organs they affect (e.g. Lung channel) or after their special functions (governing vessel). The number of acupuncture points along each of the channels varies; the heart channel has only nine points (lowest number) while the urinary bladder channel has sixty-seven points (highest number). Channels

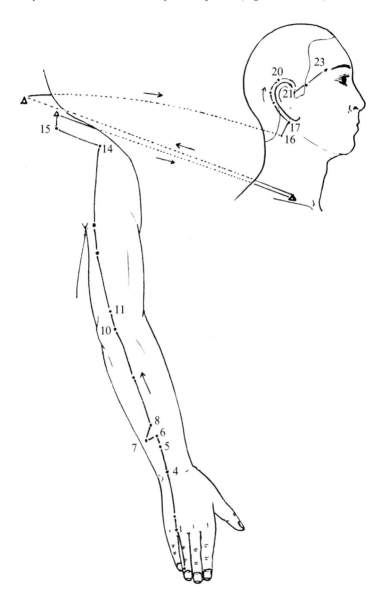

Figure 16: The three heater channel of hand-*Shaoyang*

and collaterals form a network covering the whole body, where *Qi* and blood circulate continuously to nourish all the tissues and organs. Channels and collaterals are also responsible for occurrence and transmission of diseases.

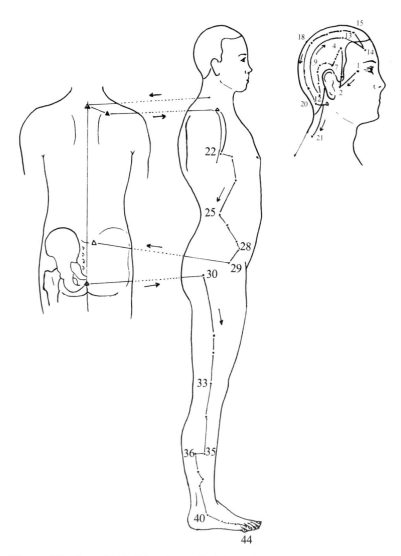

Figure 17: The gall bladder channel of foot-*Shaoyang*

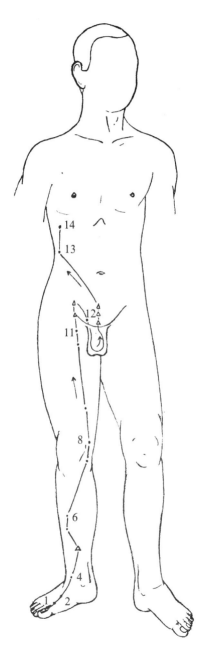

Figure 18: The liver channel of foot-*Jueyin*

C | ACUPUNCTURE & MOXIBUSTION

channels and collaterals disharmony symptom complexes, diagnosis based on [*Jing luo bian zheng* 经 络 辨 证 *King lộ biện chứng*], since the main or regular channels connect with and pertain to the **internal organs,** disorders of the channels may affect the corresponding internal organs and conversely, disorders of the internal organs will be reflected at the corresponding channels. Thus, the diagnosis of the diseases of the channels can be made by observing the location and the characteristics of the symptoms and signs. The main pathological manifestations of disharmony symptom complexes of the twelve main channels and the eight extra channels are as follows:

I. *Pathological manifestations of the twelve main channels:*

lung: cough, asthma, hemoptysis, sore throat, chest fullness, pain in the supraclavicular fossa, shoulder, back;

large intestine: epistaxis, toothache, sore throat, pain in the neck, anterior part of the shoulder, borborygmus, abdominal pain, diarrhoea;

stomach: borborygmus, abdominal pain, abdominal distension, vomiting;

spleen: belching, vomiting, epigastric pain, loose stools, jaundice;

heart: cardialgia, palpitation, insomnia, night sweating;

small intestine: deafness, yellow sclera, pain and distension of the lower abdomen;

urinary bladder: enuresis, urinary retention, rhinitis, headache, nape pain, upper and lower back pain;

kidney: enuresis, frequency, nocturnal emission, impotence, lumbago, weakness in lower limbs;

pericardium: cardialgia, palpitation, mental restlessness;

three heater: abdominal distension, oedema, enuresis, deafness, tinnitus, dysuria;

gall bladder: headache, blurred vision, pain in the supraclavicular fossa, hypochondriac pain;

liver: low back pain, lower abdominal pain, hiccup, enuresis, mental disturbance.

II. *Pathological manifestations of the eight extra channels:*

governing vessel: headache, stiffness and pain of the spine;

conception vessel: leucorrhea, irregular menstruation, hernia, urinary retention, epigastric and lower abdominal pain;

penetrating (*Chong*) **channel:**	abdominal pain, spasm of the abdominal muscles;
girdle (*Dai*) **channel:**	abdominal pain, lumbago, leucorrhea;
Yang **heel** (*Qiao*) **channel:**	epilepsy, insomnia;
Yin **heel** (*Qiao*) **channel:**	hypersomnia;
Yang **tie** (*Wei*) **channel:**	chills, fever;
Yin **tie** (*Wei*) **channel:**	cardialgia.

---

channel *Qi* [*Jing Qi* 经气 *Kinh khi*], may refer to: the vital energy or *Qi* moving in the channels; all energy integrated into a physiological cycle; the vital function of the channel.

---

channel syndrome [*Jing zheng* 经证 *Kinh chú'ng*], is one which is confined to the channel after being attacked by the pathogenic factors while the corresponding **internal organ** is not yet affected.

Chen Shi-Gong (AD **1555-1636**) [陈实功 *Trân thiệt Công*], was the distinguished surgeon and author of the *Orthodox Manual of Surgery* (*Wai ke zheng zong*) published in AD 1617, in which he set up a moral code, the **Five Don'ts** (*Wu jie*) for medical practitioners (see **five don'ts**).

---

chest, central part [*Shan zhong* 膻中 *Chiên trung*], is the name of the acupuncture point Cv17, located on the midline of the sternum, between the nipples and indicated in asthma, hiccup, chest pain and lactation deficiency. The terms Shan and Zhong mean the smell of mutton and centre respectively. In anatomy, the term '*Shan zhong*' refers to the area located between the nipples (see **sea of Qi**).

Chi, see *Qi*.

---

child, see **mother-child relationship**.

chirology, medical palmistry [*Yi xue shou xiang shu* 医学手相术 *Y học thủ tu'ó'ng thuật*], is the method of diagnosing diseases by examining the fingers and palm of the hand. According to traditional Chinese medicine, since six of the twelve main channels end or begin at the corner of the finger-nail bed, the examination of the changes in the fingers and palm of the hand may be used for the diagnosis.

Chong **channel**, see **penetrating channel.**

---

choppy pulse [*Se mai* 涩脉 *Sác mạch*], is hesitant, feeble, thready, indicating deficiency or stagnation of *Qi* and **blood.**

Classic of Acupuncture and Moxibustion [*Zhen jiu jia yi jing* 针灸甲乙经 *Châm cu'ú' Giáp Âí kinh*], is the earliest book on acupuncture and moxibustion written by Huangfu Mi (AD 214-282) which appeared in AD 259, establishing the names and number of points of each channel and their exact locations. The book also deals with the properties and indications of each acupuncture point and the methods of manipulation.

---

classical prescriptions [*Jing fang* 经方 *Kinh phu'o'ng*], recorded in *Canon of Medicine* (*Nei Jing*) and those recommended by the great physician Zhang Ji (AD 150?-219?).

---

clean [*Qing* 清 *Thanh*], 'Qing' means clean, pure, clear, contrary to dirty, polluted or *Zhuo* (e.g. *Qing Qi*: clean *Qi*).

---

clean *Qi* [*Qing Qi* 清气 *Thanh khí*], refers to: fresh air from the atmosphere; or the clarified thin part of the essence of food to be carried up into the **lungs** and then distributed to the **internal organs.**

---

coalescent points [*Tong xue* 同穴 *Dồng huyệt*], or **common points** are shared by the six extra channels, **penetrating** (*Chong*), **girdle** (*Dai*), *Yang* and *Yin* **heel** (*Qiao*), *Yang* and *Yin* **tie** (*Wei*) which have no superficial independent points of their own. They have to share a number of points with the twelve main or regular channels.

extra channels	number of coalescent points
Penetrating (*Chong*)	12
Girdle (*Dai*)	3
Yang **heel** (*Qiao*)	12
Yin **heel** (*Qiao*)	2
Yang **tie** (*Wei*)	16
Yin **tie** (*Wei*)	7

cold [*Han* 寒 *Hàn*], is one of the six atmospheric or **exogenous factors** (*Liu Qi*) which, if in excess, will become pathogenic (*Liu Yin*). It is a *Yin* phenomenon and may cause contraction of channels and collaterals and delay of circulation of *Qi* and **blood** with symptoms of numbness in the extremities, chills and anhydrosis due to blocked pores.

There are two types of cold:

1. external cold (*Wai Han*): the pathogenic factor comes from outside the body, consumes *Yang Qi*, causing chills, fever, headache.

2. internal cold (*Nei Han*): depletion of *Yang Qi* results in the invasion of external cold affecting the **spleen, kidneys, lungs** with manifestations such as diarrhoea, vomiting, abdominal pain, cold limbs, intolerance to cold, slow and deep pulse, pallor, pale tongue.

cold-heat guiding symptom complexes, diagnosis based on [*Han Re bian zheng* 寒 热 辨 证 *Hàn nhiệt biện chú'ng*], are two of the eight guiding symptom complexes used in diagnosis. Diseases caused by pathogenic heat, summer heat or dryness are mostly heat syndromes: high fever, flushed face, thirst, delirium, constipation, rapid pulse of the excess (*Shi*) type, red tongue with yellow coating. Pathogenic cold causes mostly cold syndromes: chills, cold limbs, loose stools, deep slow pulse of the excess (*Shi*) type, pale tongue with white or thick sticky coating.

cold stomach [*Wei han* 胃 寒 *Vị hàn*], shows a deficiency of *Yang*. The patient may vomit watery fluid, feels tastelessness in the mouth, cold over the stomach, prefers hot drinks.

collapse [*Tuo zheng* 脱证 *Thoát chú'ng*], due to exhaustion of *Qi* or **blood,** symptoms are cold limbs, urinary incontinence, stool incontinence, profuse sweating, open mouth, relaxed palms, fine and thready or even undetectable pulse.

---

collapsed *Qi* [*Qi xian* 气陷 *Khí hām*], is a condition in which *Qi* is so insufficient that it can no longer hold organs in place causing disorders such as prolapse of the uterus, haemorrhoids.

---

collaterals, see **channels and collaterals.**

---

combining (*He-sea*) points [*He xue* 合穴 *Hiệp huyệt*], one of the **five transporting (*Shu*) points** indicated in disorders of the intestine, stomach and other *Fu* organs. On the three *Yang* channels of foot, there are six combining points called lower combining points particularly prescribed in diseases of the six *Fu* organs (Table 2; Fig. 19).

---

common cold [*Shang feng* 伤风 *Thu'o'ng phong*], the term in Chinese literally means injured by evil cold. The exogenous wind cold or wind heat prevents the dispersing function of the lungs and weakens the defensive vital function of the superficial portion of the body.

There are two types of common cold: common cold caused by wind cold — the symptoms are chills, fever, anhydrosis, headache, nasal obstruction, cough; and common cold due to wind heat — fever, intolerance to wind, hydrosis, cough, and sore throat are the main symptoms.

---

compatibility and antagonism [*Xiang sheng xiang ke* 相生相剋 *Tu'o'ng sinh tu'o'ng khác*], is the interpromoting and counteracting relation of the five evolutive phases (see **five phases**).

Table 2: The lower combining (*He-sea*) points of the six *Fu* organs

YANG CHANNELS OF FOOT	ORGANS	COMBINING POINTS
Foot-*Yangming*	Stomach	St36 (*Zusanli*)
	Large intestine	St37 (*Shangjuxu*)
	Small intestine	St39 (*Xiajuxu*)
Foot-*Shaoyang*	Gall bladder	GB34 (*Yanglingquan*)
Foot-*Taiyang*	Urinary bladder	UB40 (*Weizhong*)
	Three heater	UB39 (*Weiyang*)

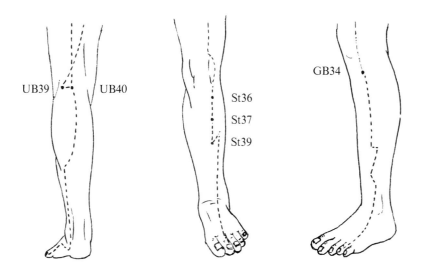

Figure 19: Lower combining (*He-sea*) points of the six *Fu* organs

Compendium of Acupuncture and Moxibustion [*Zhen jiu da cheng* 針灸大成 *Châm cứu đại thành*], a comprehensive and practical book written by Yang Ji-zhou (AD 1522-1620) in 1601, in which, the author tried to clarify the confusing state of acupuncture points and channels and to unify the divergent views concerning them. The use of moxibustion applied on the ear apex to treat cataract was also mentioned in this book.

Compendium of Materia Medica [*Ben cao gang mu* 本草纲目 *Bàn thảo cu'o'ng mục*], a comprehensive work compiled by Li Shi-zhen (AD 1518-1593) and published in 1590 in fifty-two volumes, it listed 1892 medical substances, and more than 10,000 prescriptions. The compendium was also a comprehensive work on various branches of natural history, including botany, zoology, mineralogy and metallurgy.

---

complexion [*Se* 色 *Sǎć*], or natural colouring of the face is one of the ten important points of inspection, playing an important role in the diagnosis of diseases in traditional Chinese medicine. The colour of the face and its moistness depend on the *Qi* and **blood.** 'Qi and blood of the channels flow upward into the face.' In general, the healthy person's face is shiny and moist. Abnormal complexion may reveal diseases of some internal organs:
dark complexion is associated with kidney deficiency;
blue-green complexion, sign of stagnation and obstruction of *Qi* and blood, is usually associated with liver disorders;
white complexion indicates lung diseases;
crimson complexion relates to heart diseases;
yellow complexion is particularly related to internal **dampness** caused by a weak spleen.

---

conception (Ren) vessel [*Ren mai* 任脉 *Nhậm mạch*], the term '*Ren*' means responsibility, probably the responsibility of this channel to all the *Yin* channels. This term has the connotation of conception or pregnancy since this channel arises in the uterus (Fig. 20). Diseases such as hernia, dysfunction of the visceral organs, and general debility may be attributed to the dysfunction of the conception vessel.

---

confined pulse [*Lao mai* 牢脉 *Lao mạch*], is a deep, strong and slightly taut pulse, felt only by hard pressure and usually seen in cases of accumulation of Cold factor.

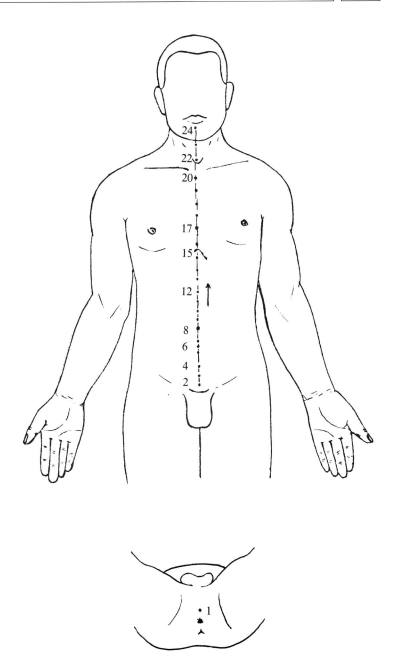

Figure 20: The conception (*Ren*) vessel

C | ACUPUNCTURE & MOXIBUSTION

confluent points, eight [*Ba mai jiao hui xue* 八脈交会穴 *Bát mạch giao hội huyệt*], are points in the extremities connecting the eight extra channels to the twelve regular channels (Table 3). These points are prescribed in diseases of the extra channels and their related regular channels, either separately according to their related channels or in conjunction with points of the lower extremities if it is the case of points of the upper extremities, or points of the upper extremities if it is the case of points of the lower extremities.

Table 3: The eight confluent points of the eight extra channels

CONFLUENT POINTS	REGULAR CHANNELS	EXTRA CHANNELS	INDICATIONS
P6 (*Neiguan*)	Pericardium	*Yin* tie (*Wei*)	Heart, chest, stomach.
Sp4 (*Gongsun*)	Spleen	penetrating (*Chong*)	
SI3 (*Houxi*)	Small intestine	governing (*Du*)	Neck, shoulder, back, inner canthus.
UB62 (*Shenmai*)	Urinary bladder	*Yang* heel (*Qiao*)	
TH5 (*Waiguan*)	Three heater	*Yang* tie (*Wei*)	Retroauricle, cheek.
GB41 (foot *Linqi*)	Gall bladder	girdle (*Dai*)	
Lu7 (*Lieque*)	Lung	conception (*Ren*)	Throat, chest, lung.
K6 (*Zhaohai*)	Kidney	*Yin* heel (*Qiao*)	

connecting (*Luo*) points [*Luo xue* 络穴 *Lạc (Lộ) huyệt*], 'Luo' means something resembling a net, or to hold something in place with a net. Each of the twelve regular channels has a collateral in the extremities connecting a definite pair of *Yin* and *Yang* channels. The point that connects the channel to its collateral is called connecting point.

There are fifteen connecting points in all: twelve related to the regular channels, two to the **conception** and **governing** vessels and one called the major connecting point of the spleen (Table 5; Fig. 21). Channels and collaterals form a network where *Qi* and **blood** circulate continuously. The connecting (*Luo*) points are prescribed in diseases involving the two

44

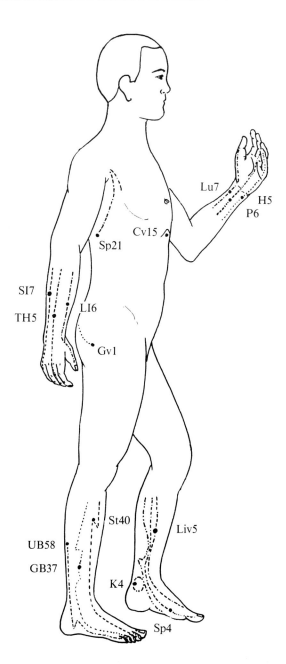

Figure 21: Connecting (*Luo*) points

Lu7

H5

P6

Cv15

Sp21

SI7

TH5

LI6

Gv1

St40

Liv5

UB58

GB37

K4

Sp4

internally externally related channels as well as diseases in the area supplied by them.

---

contraindications of acupuncture [*Jin ji zheng* 禁忌证 *Câm ky chú'ng*], are: pregnancy; any swelling, tumour sites; skin infection; presence of a cardiac pacemaker; coexisting haemorrhagic diathesis such as haemophilia; certain points located close to the vital organs or large blood vessels, e.g. St1, Cv15, Sp11. It is also advisable to delay giving acupuncture treatment to patients who are either hungry or have over-eaten, are intoxicated or exhausted (see **five depletions**).

---

convulsions, infantile [*Jing feng* 惊风 *Kinh phong*], are believed to be caused by the acute attack of **evil wind** (*Feng*) or by fright (*Jing*).

There are two types of infantile convulsions:

1. *acute* due to endogenous **wind**. Acute febrile diseases may lead to acute convulsions;

2. *chronic* due to weakness of the **spleen** and **stomach** after chronic wasting diseases.

---

cough [*Sou* 嗽 *Thâú*], can be caused by: *Exogenous* factors such as **wind cold** or **wind heat** which prevents the **lung** from performing its function of dispersing; and *endogenous* factors, a) the **lung** becomes dry due to the deficiency of *Yin* thus impairing its descending function; b) the accumulation of **damp** and the formation of **phlegm** caused by the deficiency of the **spleen** *Yang*.

---

cupping therapy [*Ba guan liao fa* 拨罐疗法 *Bạt quán liệu pháp*], is a very old and popular therapeutic method still in use by alternative healers in some countries in Europe and specially in many parts of Asia. The cups or small jars are made of metal, glass, wood or bamboo (Figure 22) in which a vacuum is created by introducing heat in the form of an ignited alcohol soaked cotton ball (for glass or metal cups) or by boiling (for wooden or bamboo cups). The cups or jars are then applied to the selected area with or without scarification on it. As the cups cool, they become firmly attached to the skin and suck blood into the cups (in case with scarifications) and cause a bruise the size of the orifice of the cup or jar. It is believed that the dark blood thus removed contains the toxins causing the diseases. Like **moxibustion,** cupping is particularly prescribed in diseases of cold: common cold, bronchitis, rheumatism, arthralgia etc. It is not advisable to use cupping in convulsions, allergic skin conditions, oedema, haemorrhagic tendency.

Figure 22: Glass inspirators for cupping therapy

---

cutaneous acupuncture, see **plum blossom acupuncture.**

D

---

dai channel, see **girdle channel.**

---

damp phlegm [*Shi tan* 湿痰 *Thấp dàm*], is produced by long standing retention of **dampness** due to the deficiency of the spleen *Qi*.

dampness [*Shi* 湿 *Thấp*], is one of the six exogenous pathogenic factors attacking the organism and impairing the normal flow of *Qi* and the normal functioning of the stomach and the intestine. This *Yang* phenomenon occurs mainly in the late summer rainy season and is characterized by: *heaviness and turbidity*, sensation of distension in the head, dizziness, general lassitude, sensation of fullness in the chest and epigastric region, nausea, vomiting; *viscosity and stagnation*, diseases caused by dampness are often lingering, e.g. rheumatism, rheumatoid arthritis, certain forms of eczema.

deep pulse [*Chen mai* 沉脉 *Trầm mạch*], is felt only upon heavy pressure, indicating the deep location of the disease.

defensive *Qi*, see *Qi*.

deficiency-excess guiding symptom complexes, diagnosis based on [*Xu shi bian zheng* 虚实辨证 *Hụ' thiệt biện chú'ng:*], 'Xu' literally means false, deficiency, 'Shi' means real, excess. *Xu* and *Shi* deficiency and excess respectively are two symptom complexes used for analysing and differentiating the pathological conditions (see **eight guiding symptom complexes of diagnosis**).

Deficiency (Xu) symptom complex: long standing diseases with signs and symptoms such as pallor, palpitation, insomnia, poor memory, night sweating, thready pulse of the deficiency type, pale tongue with thin coating.

Excess (Shi) symptom complex: recent diseases with signs and symptoms such as red face, coarse breathing, sensation of fullness in the chest, abdominal pain, constipation. The pulse is of the excess type. The tongue is red with thick coating.

diabetes [*Xiao ke bing* 消渴病 *Tang niao bing* 糖尿病 *Tiêu khát bệnh, Du'ò'ng niêú bệnh*], in traditional Chinese medicine, is either called *Xiao ke bing* (wasting and thirsting disease) or *Tang niao bing* (sugar urine disease). There are three types of diabetes: upper, middle and lower diabetes depending on the importance of any of the three symptoms, thirst, hunger, polyuria.

---

diaphragm [*Ge* 膈 *Cách*], according to traditional Chinese medicine, prevents **evil wind,** product of digestion, from moving upward to pollute the lungs and the heart. Some patients, in spite of their good appetite, still remain thin. This is due to the exhaustion of the diaphragm caused by diseases arising from overwork. The acupuncture point UB46 (*Geguan* or diaphragm barrier) is indicated in vomiting, belching, difficulty in swallowing. The point UB17 (*Geshu* or diaphragm *Shu*) is effective in vomiting, hiccup, difficulty in swallowing, asthma, cough.

Difficult Classic [*Nan jing* 难 经 *Nan kinh*], a treatise, appeared in the first or second century BC, consists of explanations of eighty-one difficult passages selected from the *Canon of Medicine* (*Nei Jing*). Its authorship is unknown though tradition ascribed it to Qin Yue-ren. The points of acupuncture and moxibustion, the method of needling, the psychological and pathological conditions of the channels and collaterals, the method of feeling the pulse were explained in detail.

---

direct hit, internal [*Zhi zhong* 直中 *Trực trung*], direct attack of the exogenous pathogenic factors on the three *Yin* channels instead of indirectly through the three *Yang* channels; or direct attack of the exogenous pathogenic factors on the internal organs.

---

direct moxibustion [*Zhi jie jiu* 直 接 灸 *Trực tiếp cu'ú'*], is performed by placing the ignited moxa cone directly over the selected point. There are two methods: *scarring moxibustion or cauterization*, the skin is burned to form blisters and ulcers with scars remaining, indicated in chronic diseases such as asthma but this method is discredited because of pain and unsightly scars; *non-scarring moxibustion*, the moxa cone is removed when half or two-thirds of it is burnt. This method is used in asthma, chronic diarrhoea, indigestion.

---

distinct channels, divergent channels [*Bie jing* 别经 *Biệt kinh*], instead of running up to the head like the six *Yang* regular channels, the six *Yin* regular channels end in the chest region near the shoulder. This lack of regular *Yin* channels in the head is overcome by the special structure called distinct or divergent channels ('*Bie*' means distinct, separate). Each pair of regular channels, e.g. lung and large intestine channels, has two distinct channels (one *Yin* for the lung channel and one *Yang* for the large intestine channel) which, after connecting with the other organ of the same pair (in this example, the distinct channel of the lung channel connects with the large intestine and the distinct channel of the large intestine channel connects with the lung) run upward to merge in the neck region and connect with the *Yang* channel (large intestine channel) of the pair. Then the *Yang* regular channel alone goes on into the head.

---

dizziness, see **vertigo.**

---

double tongue [*Chong she* 重舌 *Trùng thiệt*], is a tongue-like swelling of the sublingual veins caused by stagnation of blood. This condition may be due either to the accumulation of **heat** in the **heart** and **spleen** or the exposure to **wind** after heavy drinking.

---

dripping pulse [*Wu lou mai* 屋漏脉 *Ốc lậu mạch*], is one of the seven kinds of pulse indicating impending death. The pulse resembles water dripping from a roof crack.

---

dryness [*Zao* 燥 *Táo*], one of the six exogenous pathogenic factors which usually occurs in late autumn and impairs visceral essence and body fluid, causing red eyes, dry nose and lips, dry cough, constipation. Two kinds of dryness are described: *external dryness* (*Wai zao*), in cases of over-exposure, the dry atmosphere may cause dry skin and lips, broken finger nails; *internal dryness* (*Nei zao*), more serious than the external dryness, it is caused by loss of the body fluid. Symptoms are mental disturbance, emotional distress and usually appear at the late stage of febrile diseases or after excessive vomiting, profuse diarrhoea, excessive sweating or haemorrhage. The susceptible organs are: lungs, liver, kidneys and tongue.

Du **channel,** see **governing vessel.**

E

---

ears [*Er* 耳 *Nhĩ*], like the eyes and the mouth, are also important in both Chinese physiognomy and traditional Chinese medicine. The conditions of many internal organs may be reflected in the ears since all the channels meet in this sensory organ. Exhausted kidney *Jing* may be manifested by dry or contracted *black-grey* ears; *red ears* are manifestations of **heat** or/and **wind;** *purple ears* are seen in cases of **cold** or deficiency; *black ears* mean exhausted water; **damp heat** in the gall bladder is usually manifested by the presence of pus in the ears.

---

ear acupuncture [*Er zhen liao fa* 耳針療法 *Nhĩ châm liệu pháp*], is a method of treatment of diseases by stimulating certain points of the auricle with needles. This ancient therapeutic method has been recorded in *Nei Jing* and later in other medical literature such as *Compendium of Acupuncture and Moxibustion* by Yang Ji-zhou (AD 1601) regarding the treatment of cataract. Since all the channels meet in the ear, diseases of various parts of the body can be treated by needling the corresponding points on the auricle (Fig. 23). This method of treatment has developed in Europe more than twenty years ago, particularly in France with the theory of organs representation put forward by P. Nogier. According to his theory, different organs and parts of the body are represented in the specific areas of the ear which is seen as an upside down fetal position (Fig. 24). Since then, different methods have been developed such as embedding needles, and needling with electric stimulation. Ear acupuncture is now also used for analgesia in China (since 1959).

Precautions and contraindications: contraindicated in frost bite or inflammation of the auricle; not advisable in pregnancy; proper rest before and after needling particularly in aged and asthenic patients with hypertension and arteriosclerosis; needling in reclining position in case of overtired, hungry, asthenic, under stress patient; in cases of sudden pain, soreness around the needling site, lift the needle a little or remove it.

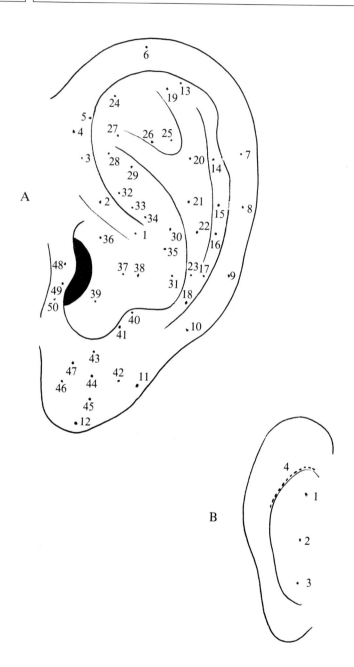

Figure 23: Distribution of auricular points

Distribution of auricular points

A. Anterior of the ear

1. Diaphragm
2. Lower rectum
3. Urethra
4. External genitalia
5. Sympathetic nerve
6. Ear apex
7. Helix 1
8. Helix 2
9. Helix 3
10. Helix 4
11. Helix 5
12. Helix 6
13. Finger
14. Wrist
15. Elbow
16. Shoulder
17. Shoulder joint
18. Clavicle
19. Ankle
20. Knee
21. Abdomen
22. Chest
23. Cervical vertebrae
24. Uterus
25. Spirit gate (*Shenmen*)
26. Femoral joint
27. Sciatic nerve
28. Urinary bladder
29. Kidney
30. Liver
31. Spleen
32. Large intestine
33. Appendix
34. Small intestine
35. Stomach
36. Oesophagus
37. Heart
38. Lung
39. Three heater
40. Relief asthma
41. Testis (Ovary)
42. Internal ear
43. Tongue
44. Eye
45. Tonsil
46. Lower tooth
47. Upper tooth
48. Pharynx
49. Adrenal
50. Internal nose

B. Posterior of the ear

1. Upper portion of the back
2. Middle portion of the back
3. Lower portion of the back
4. Groove for lowering blood pressure

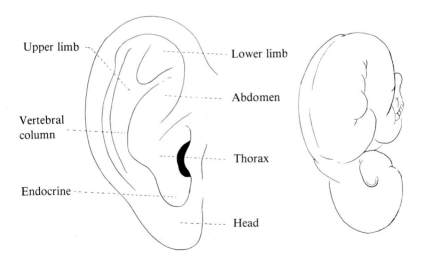

Figure 24: The representation of the body on the ear

earth [*Tu* 土 *Thô'*], one of the **five phases,** symbolizing the **spleen** and is considered the origin of everything. According to the theory of five phases, earth (spleen) promotes metal (lung), acts on water (kidney) and counteracts wood (liver) (see **five phases**).

eczema [*Shi zhen* 湿疹 *Thâp sang*], caused by **evil damp wind** when it escapes through the skin. Other name: *Shi Qi* (Damp *Qi*).

eight guiding symptom complexes of diagnosis [*Ba gang bian zheng* 八 纲 辨 证 *Bát cu'o'ng biện chú'ng*], constitute one of the three principal methods for analysing and differentiating pathological conditions. The two other methods of diagnosis are based on the theory of internal organs (*Zang Fu*) and the theory of channels and collaterals. The various signs and symptoms collected by the **four methods of diagnosis** (see **four methods of diagnosis**) are divided into four principal categories. Each category is composed of two opposite groups of symptom complexes. These eight groups of symptom complexes constitute the eight guiding symptom complexes used in diagnosis. The four pairs of symptom complexes are: external-internal; cold-heat; deficiency-excess; *Yin-Yang*. Since patients usually have a complex mixture of *Yin-Yang*, signs and symptoms, an accurate diagnosis can be reached only by combination of these eight guiding patterns.

eight joints [*Ba xi* 八溪 *Bát khê*], are the elbow, wrist, knee and ankle joints.

eight therapeutic methods [*Ba fa* 八法 *Bát pháp*], are: perspiration, emesis, purgation, mediation, invigoration, heat reduction, tonification, resolution.

eight trigrams [*Ba gua* 八卦 *Bát quái*], form a pictorial representation of the Chinese universalistic philosophy (Figure 25). The trigram or *Gua* is one of the eight basic combinations of three lines: all continuous, all broken or a combination of continuous and broken lines, joined in pair to form the sixty-four hexagrams. According to common belief, the eight trigrams were invented by Emperor Fu Hshi (about 2800 BC) but probably they were the brainchild of Wen Wang, author of the *Book of Changes* (*Yi Jing*).

Figure 25: The eight trigrams and the Taoist symbol representing the balance of *Yin* and *Yang*.

eight winds [*Ba feng* 八风 *Bát phong*], refer to the winds coming from eight different directions and causing the numbness of the skin, flesh, muscles, bones and pulse. It is also the name of eight extraordinary acupuncture points located on the dorsum of foot, on the webs between the five toes and indicated in beri-beri, redness and swelling of the dorsum of foot.

electro-acupuncture [*Dian zhen* 电 针 *Diện châm*], is a method of acupuncture using electricity for point stimulation. Louis Berlioz, a French physician, was the first to report the potentiating effects of electro-acupuncture in 1816. In 1825, Sarlandière, also in France, used this method to treat diseases such as gout and rheumatism. Later, before the Second World War, Niboyet in France demonstrated that the acupuncture points are areas of low electrical resistance. If an organ or tissue deep in the body is affected, the corresponding points on the surface of the body will show an altered electromotive force. Since then, a variety of electrical apparatus has been developed to measure the skin's electrical resistance and conductance over the acupuncture points. In West Germany, R. Voll has developed an electro-acupuncture machine (Figure 26) based upon this principle. Nakatani (1950) in Japan, developed a system of acupuncture similar to that of R. Voll and called it Ryodoraku.

Figure 26: Electro-acupuncture therapy apparatus

empty pulse [*Xu mai* 虚脉 *Hu' mạch*], floating, feeble pulse seen in case of deficiency of *Qi* and **blood.**

---

endogenous factors [*Nei yin* 内因 *Nội nhân*], refers mainly to the seven excessive emotional factors (see **seven emotions**).

---

endorphins, in 1970, experiments performed on rabbits in China revealed the existence of certain pain-reducing substances which could be transmitted from one animal's cerebrospinal fluid to another's. Five years later, American and British works confirmed the existence of the morphine-like substances in the central nervous system and many other parts of the body. These substances were named endorphins (ENDOgenous and moRPHINE). In patients suffering from chronic pain, the endorphins level in the fluid around the brain and in the cerebrospinal fluid is low. Acupuncture increases the endorphins level and therefore blocks pain. This analgesic effect can be blocked by Naloxone, a morphine antagonist.

---

enuresis [*Yi ni* 遗溺 *Di niêú*], is considered abnormal if it occurs in children over three years old or in adults. It is caused by insufficient kidney *Qi* and by weakness of the **urinary bladder** in controlling urination.

---

environment [*Huan jing* 环境 *Hoàn cảnh*], in traditional Chinese medicine, this term does not necessarily refer to the external environmental factors; it could be either the exogenous factors such as **wind, heat, dampness, dryness** etc., or the endogenous factors such as emotions, feelings etc.

Epidemic Febrile Diseases, Treatise on [*Wen yi lun* 温疫论 *Ôn dịch luận*], is a study of etiology and pathology of epidemic febrile diseases in two volumes, published in AD 1642 by Wu You-xing (AD 1582-1652).

---

essence of life [*Jing* 精 *Jing Qi* 精气 *Tinh, Tinh khí*], a fundamental substance which is a basis for all organic life. Jing, one of the basic concepts in traditional Chinese medicine. There are two types of essence of life: *Reproductive essence*, represented in men by the spermatoza and in women by the ova; and *Nutritive essence*, fundamental substance which forms the human body and maintains the body functions. The essence of life has two sources: *congenital* essence inherited from parents; and *acquired* essence derived from the purified parts of ingested food. When in excess, it is believed that the essence of life is stored in the kidneys. The terms *Jing* and *Qi* are sometimes used together since *Jing* is *Yin* and *Qi* is *Yang* and they are mutually dependent.

---

exhaustion of *Yang* [*Tuo Yang* 脱阳 *Thoát Du'o'ng*], in the body will increase the *Yin* factor with symptoms such as *illusio optica*, illusion. This term refers also to the state of exhaustion in the male after sexual intercourse.

---

exhaustion of *Yin* [*Tuo Yin* 脱阴 *Thoát Âm*], exhaustion of *Yin* of the viscera specially of the **liver** and **kidneys** will cause sudden loss of vision. This condition is usually seen in case of malnutrition, post-partum asthenia.

---

exogenous pathogenic factors, six, see **six excessive atmospheric influences.**

---

exterior interior guiding symptom complexes, diagnosis based on [*Biao li bian zheng* 表里辨证 *Biêủ lý biện chú'ng*], shows the relative location of the affected area and the direction of development of the disease. *Exterior symptom complex (Biao zheng)*: refers to diseases caused by invasion of the superficial portion of the body by the exogenous pathogenic factors. The diseases are usually mild and superficial with main manifestations such as sudden onset, intolerance to cold or wind, fever, headache, nasal obstruction, superficial pulse. *Interior symptom complex*

(*Li zheng*): Diseases may result either from transmission of the exogenous pathogenic factors to the interior or direct attack on *Zang Fu* organs by the exogenous factors. Dysfunction of the internal organs (*Zang Fu*) is also among the causes of the interior symptom complex. Symptoms are high fever, thirst, delirium, vomiting, deep pulse.

---

extra channels, eight [*Qi jing ba mai* 奇经八脉 *Kỳ kinh bát mạch*], also translated as odd meridians, curious meridians, irregular vessels, marvellous vessels (marvellous results in chronic diseases when acupuncture therapy on twelve regular channels failed), they are the **governing** (*Du*), **conception** (*Ren*), **penetrating** (*Chong*), **girdle** (*Dai*), *Yang* heel (*Qiao*), *Yin* heel, *Yang* tie (*Wei*), *Yin* tie channels. Their courses of distribution are different from those of the twelve regular channels and they do not connect with the internal (*Zang Fu*) organs (thus the name odd or curious channels). All but two of them (**governing** and **conception vessels**) have no acupuncture points of their own. They have instead common points with other regular channels (see **coalescent points**). The extra channels act as safety valves: when there is an excess of flow of *Qi* and **blood,** they act as the drains in bypassing the flow.

---

extraordinary organs [*Qi hang zhi fu* 奇恒之府 *Kỳ hằng chi phủ*] the **brain, marrow, bone, uterus, blood vessels** and **gall bladder,** are so-called since they resemble the *Yang* organs but have the function of the *Yin* organs. Since they are dependent on the primary organs, in case of disease, only the primary organs are to be treated. For example, disorders of the blood vessels may be treated through other organs such as the **heart, liver** or **spleen;** diseases of the brain, marrow or bones may be treated through the **kidney** or the kidney channel.

---

extraordinary points [*Jing wai qi xue* 经外奇穴 *Kinh ngoại kỳ huyệt*],   are so-called as they were discovered in the course of practice, and have definite locations but are not listed in the system of the fourteen channels.

---

eyes [*Yan* 眼 *Nhãn*],   according to the Chinese and Vietnamese physiognomies, are the windows of the soul and are very important since they reflect people's characters and the futures. 'When people sleeps, Shen stays in the heart, when people awakes, Shen moves to the eyes.' Traditional Chinese medicine considers the eyes as the mirror of the patient's state of health. All the organs have a more or less certain influence on the function of the eyes. 'Pure *Jing Qi* of all organs flows to the eyes.' *Alert eyes* indicate intact *Jing*. *Sluggish eyes* mean either **wind** or deficient condition. **Heat** condition is manifested by the *congested whites* of the eyes. *Excessive lacrimation* is usually a sign of **liver** fire. *Dilated pupils* indicate a serious condition, a deficient **kidney** *Yin*, a poisoning. *Fear of bright light* is the manifestation of excess.

F

facial expression, see **spirit.**

facial paralysis [*Mian shen jing ma bi* 面神经麻痹 *Diện thần kinh ma tê*], is due to perturbation of *Qi* and blood and undernourishment of the channels by invasion of pathogenic **wind cold** in the **channels** and **collaterals** of the facial region.

fainting spell during acupuncture treatment [*Yun zhen* 晕针 *Vụ'ng châm*], is usually due to the patient's nervousness or the physician's improper manipulation.

fifth watch diarrhoea [*Wu geng xie* 五更泻 *Ngũ canh tả*], occurs everyday before dawn and is caused by deficiency of **fire** in the gate of life to warm the **stomach** and **spleen.** Watch or '*Geng*' is one of the five two-hour periods into which the night was formerly divided: *first watch* from 7 p.m. to 9 p.m., *second watch* from 9 p.m. to 11 p.m., *third watch* from 11 p.m. to 1 a.m., *fourth watch* from 1 a.m. to 3 a.m., *fifth watch* from 3 a.m. to 5 a.m.

fine pulse [*Wei mai* 微脉 *Vi mạch*], a thready and soft pulse, seen in cases of extreme exhaustion.

finger puncture [*Zhi zhen liao fa* 指针疗法 *Chỉ châm liệu pháp*], an ancient method of treatment using fingers instead of needle to pinch or knock at the location of points. This method has been recorded in a medical book of the *Jin* dynasty (AD 265-420) relating to the rescue of an unconscious person by pinching at the point Gv26 (*Renzhong*).

finger veins, diagnosis based on [*Zhen zhi wen* 诊指纹 *Chẩn chỉ văn*], since six of the twelve regular channels end near or begin at the corners of the nail beds of the fingers, any change in the fingers may be suggestive of diseases of the internal organs. Based on this theory, a method of diagnosis for children under three years old has been developed by rubbing the index finger to see the extending and colour of the minor veins. *Intertwinement of the red and yellow veins* indicates healthy state. *Purplish red veins* reveal **heat**. *Purple and dark blue veins* indicate **wind, convulsions and pain** (see **three-barrier pulse**).

fire [*Huo* 火 *Hoả*], one of the **five phases** symbolizing the **heart**. According to the theory of five phases, fire (heart) promotes earth (spleen), acts on metal (lung) and counteracts water (kidney) (see **five phases**). Fire is also a *Yang* pathogenic factor like **heat** and **mild heat**. They are of the same nature but different in intensity: fire is the most severe and mild heat the least intense.

fish swimming pulse [*Yu xiang mai* 鱼翔脉 *Ngư' tu'ò'ng mạch*], so-called because it resembles a swimming fish, is one of the seven kinds of pulse indicating impending death.

five abstainings [*Wu jin* 五禁 *Ngũ cấm*], each of the five viscera relates to one of the five tastes, and if an organ is affected, one should abstain from its corresponding taste, e.g. in case of disease of the kidney, salty foods should be avoided (see **five tastes**).

five animals game method [*Wu qin xi fa* 五禽戏法 *Ngũ câm hý pháp*], is a series of physical exercises inspired by the movements of five kinds of wild animals: tiger, bear, monkey, deer and bird in flight, and was invented by Hua Tuo (AD 141-212), the famous surgeon, to treat diseases and to promote health.

---

five cereals [*Wu gu* 五谷 *Ngũ cốc*], is a term usually referring to: wheat, rice, beans, two kinds of millet. The other meanings are food and crop.

---

five colours [*Wu se* 五色 *Ngũ sắc*], are blue, yellow, red, white and black and correspond to the liver, spleen, heart, lung, kidney respectively. These five colours also suggest the kinds of diseases and their causes: *blue* colour suggests diseases of **wind, cold;** *red* colour indicates disease of **heat;** *yellow* colour suggests **dampness** and **heat, dampness** and **cold,** blood deficiency; *white* colour reveals debility and **cold** condition; *black* colour indicates cold, pain, **blood** stasis, deficiency.

---

five deficiencies [*Wu xu* 五虚 *Ngũ hu'*], refer to the deficiency of five viscera with manifestations such as thready and weak pulse, cold skin, shallow breath, diarrhoea, anorexia etc.

---

five depletions [*Wu duo* 五夺 *Ngũ doạt*], are conditions contra-indicated in acupuncture and administration of medicine: cachexia, post haemorrhage, excessive perspiration, profuse diarrhoea, repeated haemorrhages.

---

five don'ts [*Wu jie* 五戒 *Ngũ gió'i*], a moral code for physicians proposed by Chen Shi-gong (AD 1555-1636) in his *Orthodox Manual of Surgery*. 1. Don't be late when called to see a patient, be he poor or rich. Give the required medicine whether you are paid or not. 2. Don't see a girl, a widow or a nun without the presence of a third person. Never talk about what you have seen or hear to anybody even to your wife. 3. Don't substitute any precious ingredients entrusted to you in preparing the medicine. 4. Don't leave your office during office hours for pleasure trips or drinking parties. Attend to your patient in person, write the prescription carefully and clearly. 5. Don't have any immoral thoughts when you are called to see a prostitute or some person's mistress. Treat them as people of good family. Leave them as soon as you have done your duty and don't call again unless you are requested.

---

five emotions [*Wu zhi* 五志, *Ngũ chí*], are: joy, happiness (*Xi*); anger (*Nu*); anxiety (*You*); sorrow, meditation (*Si*); fear (*Kong*) and are related to the **heart, liver, spleen, lung** and **kidney** respectively. In cases of excess, these five emotions can affect the normal circulation of *Qi* and **blood**, causing damage to the related organs.

---

five evils [*Wu e* 五恶, *Ngũ ác*], are **heat, cold, wind, dampness** and **dryness**, in cases of excess, may be harmful to the **heart, lung, liver, spleen** and **kidney** respectively.

---

five excesses [*Wu shi* 五实 *Ngũ thiệt*], excess of **heat** in five viscera is manifested by symptoms such as forceful pulse, burning heat of the skin surface, abdominal distension, constipation, anuria, delirium etc.

---

five exhaustions [*Wu lao* 五劳 *Ngũ lao*], may refer to the lesions of: five *Zang* organs (**heart, liver, spleen, lung, kidney**) or, *Qi*, **blood**, flesh, **bone**, sinew or muscle.

---

five organs of sense [*Wu guan* 五濂 *Ngũ quan*], are the **nose, eyes, lips, tongue** and **ears** corresponding to five viscera, **lungs, liver, spleen, heart** and **kidneys** respectively and constitute the major observation points in diagnosis since their abnormalities indicate disorders of the corresponding organs.

---

five phases, five elements theory [*Wu xing shuo* 五行说 *Ngũ hành thuyết*], literally '*Wu*' means five and '*Xing*' refers to walk or movement. This term is usually translated as five elements. The translated term five evolutive phases or simply five phases is however more accurate. This theory is in fact, an ancient Chinese philosophical concept with a political basis (interpretation of the correct timing of rites, succession of dynasties etc). It was first systemized by Zou Wen (about 350-270 BC) and tends to classify phenomena in five categories represented by **wood, fire, earth, metal, water** and explains the relationships between them (See Table 4 and Figure 27.)

An example of this is wood is promoted by water which is the 'mother' of wood while fire or 'child' of wood is promoted by 'mother' wood. Wood overacts on earth and is acted upon by metal. When in excess, wood counteracts on metal. In cases of deficiency, wood is overacted by metal and counteracted on by earth.

Table 4: The correspondences of five phases

	WOOD	FIRE	EARTH	METAL	WATER
Zang (Yin)	Liver	Heart	Spleen	Lungs	Kidneys
Fu (Yang)	Gall bladder	Small intestine	Stomach	Large intestine	Urinary bladder
Season	Spring	Summer	Mid-Summer	Autumn	Winter
Weather	Wind	Heat	Dampness	Dryness	Cold
Colour	Green	Red	Yellow	White	Black
Odour	Rancid	Scorched	Fragrant	Rotten	Putrid
Direction	East	South	Centre	West	North
Flavour	Sour	Bitter	Sweet	Hot	Salt
Sound	Shout	Laugh	Sing	Weep	Groan
Musical note	*Chio*	*Chih*	*Kung*	*Shang*	*Yu*
Emotion	Anger	Joy	Sympathy	Grief	Fear
Meat	Chicken	Mutton	Beef	Horse	Pork
Cereal	Wheat	Glutinous millet	Millet	Rice	Beans
Orifice	Eye	Tongue	Mouth	Nose	Ear
Fluid	Tears	Sweat	Saliva	Mucus	Urine
Tissue	Ligament	Blood vessel	Muscle	Skin	Bone

Applied to traditional Chinese medicine, this theory tends to explain the aetiology, mechanism and evolution of the diseases and constitutes a guide to medical practice. For example *lung diseases* may be caused by:

disorders of the **lung** itself; disorder of the **spleen** (mother affecting child); **kidney** trouble (child affecting mother); **heart** disease (fire over-acting on metal); **liver** impairment (wood counter-acting on metal). The correspondence of five phases may also suggest the aetiology of certain diseases: *white complexion* with rotten odour suggests **lung** disease; *dark complexion* of patient suffering from heart disease suggests the action of the water (kidney) on fire (heart).

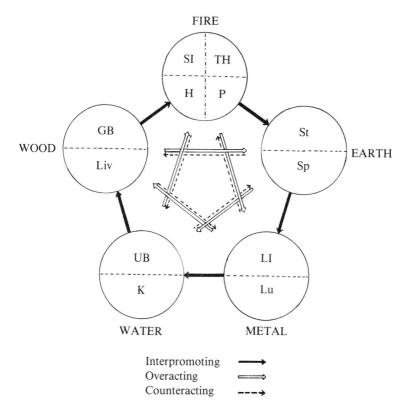

Figure 27: The relationships of the five phases

This theory of five phases and the *Yin-Yang* theory are inseparable and play an important role in traditional Chinese medicine.

---

five poisonous creatures [*Wu du* 五 毒 *Ngũ độc*],   the viper, lizard, scorpion, toad and centipede are used to counteract and to eliminate diseases or poisons. It is a therapeutic method known as 'combat poison with poison'.

---

five tastes [*Wu wei* 五味 *Ngũ vị*], there are five categories of taste and it is believed that after reaching the stomach, each of them goes to its related organ to strengthen and to nourish it.

Since there is an association of tastes with a particular organ, ingestion of certain food is not advisable in cases of disease related to that organ.

1. *Sour* moves to the **liver** and since the liver controls the **tendons** and **muscles,** in cases of diseases of the tendons and muscles, avoid sour food and drink.

2. *Bitter* moves to the **heart** and since the heart controls the **mind** and **vessels,** bitter food can injure *Qi*.

3. *Sweet* may injure the flesh since it moves to the **spleen** which controls the muscles.

4. Avoid *hot food* in case of skin and hair diseases since hot taste goes to the **lungs** which dominate the **skin** and **hair.**

5. *Salty food* is contraindicated in blood diseases since salt moves to the **kidneys** which manufacture **blood** and control the **water** metabolism.

---

five transporting (*Shu*) points [*Wu shu xue* 五俞穴 *Ngũ du huyệt*], '*Shu*' means transport or convey. There are five specific points on each of the twelve regular channels, arranged in the following order from the extremities of the limbs up to the elbow or knee: *Jing*-well, *Ying*-spring, *Shu*-stream, *Jing*-river, *He*-sea (Figure 28). These names symbolize the movement of *Qi* along the channels like the movement of water in the river from its source to the sea. Each of the five categories of transporting (*Shu*) points has the same properties:

1. *Jing*-well points are prescribed in mental diseases.

2. *Ying*-spring points are used in febrile diseases.

3. *Shu*-stream points are indicated in arthralgia caused by **evil wind** and **dampness.**

4. *Jing*-river points are effective in asthma, cough, throat diseases.

5. *He*-sea points are prescribed in disorders of the intestine, stomach and other *Fu* organs.

Each of the five transporting (*Shu*) points is attributed to an evolutive phase and, according to the theory of **five phases,** each channel has a 'mother' point and a 'child' point (Tables 5, 9). The 'mother' point which has a tonifying effect, is indicated in deficiency (*Xu*) syndrome of its related

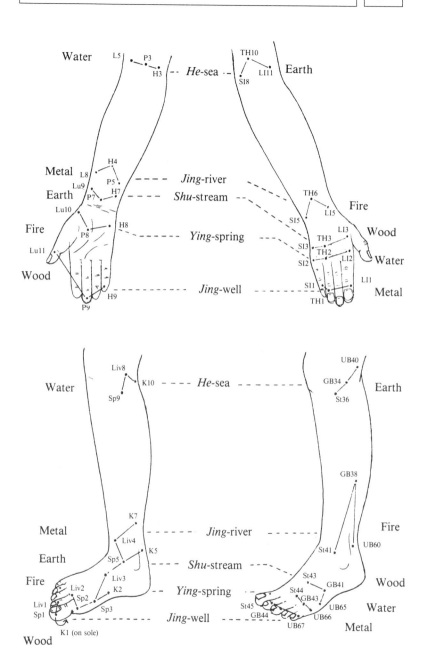

Figure 28: Five transporting (*Shu*) points

channel and the 'child' point, due to its reducing effect, is prescribed in excess (*Shi*) syndrome of its related channel. With this series of five *Shu* points, it is therefore possible to treat nearly any disease of any part of the body without using any other acupuncture points.

flaccid paralysis [*Wei zheng* 痿 证 *Nuy chứ'ng*], is caused by damage of the tendons due to: *accumulation* of **damp heat** affecting the sunlight *Yang* (*Yangming*) channels; *exhaustion* of body fluid caused by the effects of exogenous **wind-heat** on the lungs; loss of *Jing* and *Qi* of the **liver** and **kidney** after a long illness or resulting from sexual over-indulgence.

Table 5: The specific points

CHANNELS	FIVE CATEGORIES OF TRANSPORTING (*SHU*) POINTS					CONNEC-TING (*LUO*) POINT	SOURCE (*YUAN*) POINT	ALARM (FRONT *MU*) POINT	ASSOCI-ATED (BACK *SHU*) POINT
	WOOD	FIRE	EARTH	METAL	WATER				
Heart	9	8	7	4	3	5	7	Cv14	UB15
Small intestine	3	5	8	1	2	7	4	Cv4	UB27
Urinary bladder	65	60	40	67	66	58	64	Cv3	UB28
Kidney	1	2	3	7	10	4	3	GB25	UB23
Pericardium	9	8	7	5	3	6	7	Cv17	UB14
Three heater	3	6	10	1	2	5	4	Cv5	UB22
Gall bladder	41	38	34	44	43	37	40	GB24	UB19
Liver	1	2	3	4	8	5	3	Liv14	UB18
Lung	11	10	9	8	5	7	9	Lu1	UB13
Large intestine	3	5	11	1	2	6	4	St25	UB25
Stomach	43	41	36	45	44	40	42	Cv12	UB21
Spleen	1	2	3	5	9	4	3	Liv13	UB20

flicking pulse [*Tan shi mai* 弹石脉 *Dạn thạch mạch*], a deep and solid pulse resembling flicking stone with the fingertip; one of the seven pulses indicating impending death.

floating pulse [*Fu mai* 浮脉 *Phù mạch*], can be felt by light

ACUPUNCTURE & MOXIBUSTION F

touch but disappears on hard pressure, indicating that the disharmony caused by the external pernicious factor is in the superficial part of the body.

flooding pulse [*Hong mai* 洪脉 *Hồng mạch*], like dashing waves, it rises forcefully and declines gradually. Usually seen in cases with excessive **evil heat**.

fluid, body [*Jin ye* 津 液 *Tân dịch*], in traditional Chinese medicine, is not the same as that in modern physiology. According to the Chinese conception, the body fluid, other than blood, which exists in the blood and the interstices of the tissues, comes from food and drink.

There are two types of body fluid: *limpid and thin type* (*Jin*): its function is to warm and to nourish the muscles, to moisten the skin; *turbid and viscous type* (*Ye*): for lubricating the joints, toning the brain and moistening the orifices. Besides which, any excretion as well as secretion such as tear, saliva, milk, and any fluid from the genital apparatus, is also considered body fluid. Urine is not regarded as body fluid: it is only a fluid of waste matter. When the normally clear body fluid becomes turbid, there will be convulsions, cramps. In cases of invasion of the body by the **evil cold,** the body fluid becomes thinner and loses its effectiveness.

fontanelle [*Xin men* 囟门 *Thông môn*], literally means vent door, so-called since the fontanelle is regarded as a gate through which the *Hun* or the **soul** escapes at the moment of death.

four methods of diagnosis [*Si zhen fa* 四诊法 *Tú' chẩn pháp*], are inspection, listening and smelling, interrogation, and touching. According to Szuma Chien's *Historical Records*, Bian Que (about 500 BC) is believed to be the author of these four methods of diagnosis.

four seas [*Si hai* 四海 *Tú' hải*], the term 'Hai' or sea refers to the internal environment of the body. 'Man has Four Seas' which are: 1. *sea of marrow* (*Sui hai*), referring to the **brain**. 2. *sea of blood* (*Xue hai*), referring to the **penetrating** (*Chong*) **channel** which is 'the sea of twelve channels'. The **spleen** is considered a supplementary sea of blood. 3. *sea* *of air or Qi (Qi hai)*: refers to the area of the breast between the nipples (around Cv17), and has close relationship with the **heart** and the **lungs**. Some maintain there are two seas of *Qi*, one around Cv17 called upper sea of *Qi* and the other around Cv6 called lower sea of *Qi*. 4. *sea of water and grains (Shui gu zhi hai)*: represented by the **stomach**.

---

front-*Mu* points, see **alarm points.**

---

front private parts [*Qian yin* 前阴 *Tiên âm*], refers to the external genitalia including the external orifice of the urethra.

Fu Hshi [伏羲 *Phục Hy*], the first of the three emperors, lived about 2800 BC (see **synopsis of Chinese medical history**). He taught his subjects fishing, domestication of animals, hunting and breeding silkworms. The inventions of the calendar, musical instruments and **eight trigrams** (*Ba Gua*) are also attributed to him.

Fu **organs,** see **internal organs.**

---

full pulse [*Shi mai* 实脉 *Thiệt mạch*], a forceful pulse felt on both light and heavy pressure, seen in cases of accumulation of excessive **heat** in the interior.

G

---

gall bladder [*Dan nang* 胆囊 *Dảm nang*], one of the six *Fu* organs whose main function is to store bile and excrete it continuously to the intestine for the digestion of food. The function of the gall bladder is closely related to that of the **liver**: both can generate **fire** which may be the cause of many disorders. Like the liver, the gall bladder is the symbol of courage.

ACUPUNCTURE & MOXIBUSTION G

If someone is bold, courageous, he is said to have big liver and big gall bladder. The term '*Gan Dan*' (liver-gall bladder) means courageous, fearless.

gate of life [*Ming men* 命门 *Mệnh môn*], like the **three-heater,** is difficult to define. Both are identified by function rather than by structure. This term may refer either to the right kidney or the region between the two kidneys where the sperm is generated in males and the function of the uterus is performed in females. The lack of **fire** of the gate of life due to deficiency of the original vital function is manifested by symptoms such as lassitude, chills in the back, lumbago, impotence, nocturnal emission. Sexual hyperaesthesia, insomnia, dreamfulness etc. are manifestations of the intense **fire** of the gate of life which is usually due to the deficiency of the kidney *Yin*. The acupuncture point Gv4 (*Mingmen*) is indicated in lumbago, impotence, nocturnal emission.

gauge [*Xing hao* 型号 *Hình hiệu*], acupuncture needles are of different sizes. The most commonly used are as follows:

| Gauge: | 26 | 28 | 30 | 32 |
| Diameter mm: | 0.46 | 0.38 | 0.32 | 0.26 |

general check-up [*Quan shen bian zhen fa* 全身遍诊法 *Toàn thân biện chứ'ng pháp*], doesn't refer to the general examination as in Western medicine, it refers simply to the traditional method of feeling the pulse in Chinese medicine. Since the pulse, with its three-portion and nine-area, represents the entire body, feeling it is therefore equivalent to the general check-up (see **three-portion and nine-area pulse taking method**).

Genuine meaning of the Difficult Classic [*Nan jing ben yi* 难经本义 *Nan kinh bàn nghĩa*], a most influential book among complementary works of *Difficult Classic* (*Nan Jing*), compiled by Hua Shou (AD 1304-1386) and published in AD 1361.

getting the *Qi* [*De Qi* 得气 *Dắc khí*], is indicated after the insertion of the needle, when the patient may feel soreness, distension, heaviness

71

and numbness around the insertion point. This is the normal reaction. Delay in getting the *Qi* may be due to the local obstruction of the channel. In this case, avoid forceful manipulation by using mild moxibustion or by selecting other points.

---

girdle (*Dai*) channel [*Dai mai* 带脉 *Dái mạch*], one of the eight

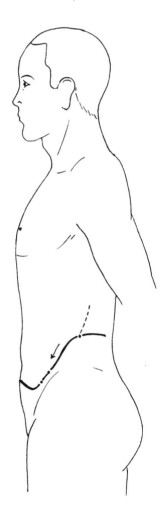

Figure 29: The girdle (*Dai*) channel

extra channels, so-called since this channel has the function of binding up all the channels and runs transversely around the waist like a belt (Figure 29). The pathological manifestations of this channel are: abdominal pain, weakness and pain of the lumbar region, leucorrhea.

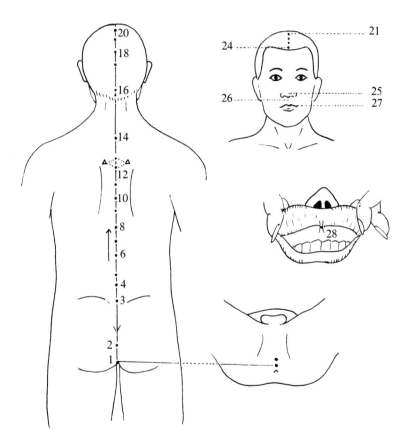

Figure 30: The governing (*Du*) vessel

governing (*Du*) vessel [*Du mai* 督脈 *Dôć mạch*],   so-called since this channel has the function of governing all the *Yang* channels (Figure 30). The pathological manifestations of this channel are stiffness and pain of the spine, opisthotonos, headache.

grain *Qi* [*Gu Qi* 谷气 *Cốc khí*], is derived from the digestion of food. The grain (*Gu*) *Qi*, the original (*Yuan*) *Qi* and the natural air (*Kong*) *Qi* form the normal or upright (*Zheng*) *Qi* to nourish the body.

---

granary [*Cang lin* 仓廪 *Thương lẫm*], refers to the stomach. Some hold that the spleen is also a granary. The acupuncture point UB50 *Weicang* (stomach granary) is indicated in abdominal distension, epigastric pain, back pain.

---

grandson channel [*Sun luo jing* 孙络经 *Tôn lạc kinh*], is the branch of the **connecting** (*Luo*) **channel** and is located in the skin. In case of excess of *Qi*, the overflow will be directed to the grandson channel, resulting in the change of the skin's colour and consistency.

---

greater *Yang* **syndrome** [*Taiyang bing* 太阳病 *Thái dương bệnh*], a condition due to the attack of **wind** and **cold** on the body surface. Symptoms are headache, chills, stiffness of the neck etc. (see **six channels, diagnosis based on**).

---

greater *Yin* **syndrome** [*Taiyin bing* 太阴病 *Thái Âm bệnh*], is the syndrome of the greater *Yin* channel relating to the **spleen**, due to the attack of **cold** and **dampness**. The main manifestations are absence of fever, abdominal distension, indigestion, poor appetite, diarrhoea, vomiting. (See **six channels, diagnosis based on**.)

---

guide tube [*Guan zhen* 管针 *Quản châm*], a supplemental instrument for easier insertion of the acupuncture needle. A thin plastic tube through which the needle will slide freely, is placed on the acupuncture point. The needle is then slipped in and tapped with the forefinger to make the initial penetration. The patient doesn't feel any pain after insertion of the needle. The size of the guiding tube depends on the length of the needle (Figure 31).

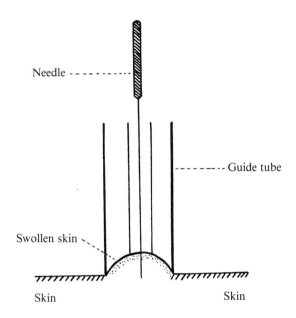

(a) Principle of the guide tube. The skin which is in touch with the edge of the tube is swollen, the patient doesn't feel any pain after insertion of the needle.

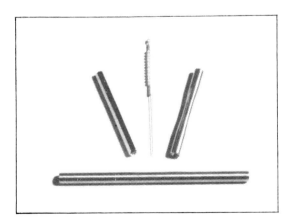

(b) Diferent sizes of guide tube.

Figure 31: Guide tubes

H

haemorrhoids [*Zhi* 痔 *Trì*], in Western medicine, are classified as internal and external according to their relationship to the anal orifice. Traditional Chinese medicine classifies haemorrhoids into twenty-four different types after their external shapes, e.g. rat tail, cherries, hanging pearl, chicken heart, lotus flower etc. Haemorrhoids are caused by extreme deficiency of *Qi* which is unable to hold organs in place. This is also the

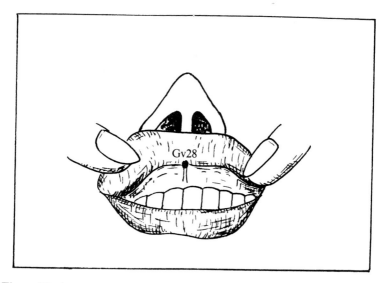

Figure 32: Acupuncture point mouth *Yinjiao* (Gv28) used in diagnosis of haemorrhoids

cause of the prolapse of the **uterus**. In ancient Japan and China, it was prohibited to examine the anus of noblemen and noblewomen. To make the diagnosis of haemorrhoids, the physician had to examine the region of the acupuncture point Gv28 (mouth *Yinjiao*), located between the upper lip and the upper labial gingiva, in the frenulum of the upper lip (Figure 32). It is said that eighty per cent of cases of haemorrhoids have small white spots in this area.

ACUPUNCTURE & MOXIBUSTION | H

hair [*Mao fa* 毛发 *Mao phát*], the terms '*Mao*' and '*Fa*' mean body hair and head hair respectively. The hair condition depends on the **lung** since the function of the lung is to distribute the essence of food to the entire body surface, giving shine to the skin, brightness and abundance to the hair. The hair on the head is also the 'mirror of the kidney' since the **kidney** *Qi* is indispensable to the development of the body. Thin, grey, falling hair are manifestations of deficient *Qi* or **blood**.

---

hand acupuncture [*Shou zhen* 手针 *Thủ châm*], a method particularly prescribed in acute conditions. The acupuncture points are selected on a symptomatic basis (Figure 33).

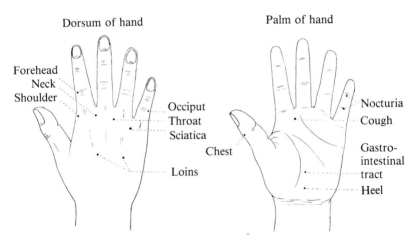

Figure 33: hand acupuncture

He-sea **points,** see **combining points.**

---

head development [*Tou* 头 *Thủ*], of the child is a good indication of the state of *Jing*, as *Jing* or essence of life controls the maturation. The deficiency of the kidney *Jing* is manifested by the abnormal size of the child's head, either larger or smaller than normal, and mental deficiency.

---

headache [*Tou tong* 头痛 *Thủ thống*], may be caused by the attack of endogenous (**head wind**) or exogenous (**wind cold**) factors resulting in the derangement of *Qi* and **blood** in the head and the delay of circulation of *Qi* in the channels that traverse the head. All the *Yang* channels of hand and foot meet in the head. *Frontal headache* is related to the **stomach channel,** *bilateral or unilateral temporal headache* relates to the **gall bladder channel,** *parietal headache* is connected with the **liver channel,** *occipital headache* corresponds to the **urinary bladder channel.** Headache is of two types: 1. *excess* (*Shi*), violent headache, vertigo, nausea; and 2. *deficiency* (*Xu*), insidious pain.

---

heart [*Xin* 心. *Tâm*], is one of the five *Zang* organs. Like the **liver,** the heart is the noblest and the most essential organ in the body. The Chinese expression 'My heart and my liver' is usually used to prove one's sincerity. The main physiological functions of the heart are: controlling **blood** and vessels; housing the **spirit** (*Shen*) thus influencing the face; opening into the **tongue** which is 'the mirror of the heart'; controlling the **kidneys.**

---

heat (fire, mild heat) [*Re* 热 *Nhiệt*], are *Yang* pathogenic factors. They are of the same nature but different in intensity: **fire** is the most severe and mild heat is the least intense. Fire is also a normal *Yang* of the body and should not be confused with the pernicious fire.

   Heat is of two types: 1. *external heat* (*Biao Re*), disharmonies are marked by symptoms and signs such as high fever, intolerance to wind, headache, thirst, irritability, delirium, rapid pulse. The onset is usually abrupt; and 2. *internal heat* (*Li Re*), caused by disharmonies of the *Yin* and *Yang* of various organs and is manifested by an insidious onset, thirst, irritability, scanty urine, redness of tongue proper with yellow coating, rapid and forceful pulse.

---

heat-stroke [*Zhong shu* 中暑 *Trúng thử*], is usually caused by invasion of **summer heat** injuring *Qi* and *Yin* in case of exhaustion after a prolonged exposure to the sun. In mild type, the symptoms are headache, perspiration, hot skin, dry tongue and mouth, superficial and rapid pulse. Loss of consciousness occurs in severe cases.

---

heel channels, see *Yang* **heel channel** and *Yin* **heel channel.**

---

hidden pulse [*Fu mai* 伏脉 *Phục mạch*],   so-called since the pulse is only felt on strong pressure as if it is embedded in the muscles. This type of pulse is seen in cases of syncope, shock, severe pain.

Historical Records [*Shi ji* 史记 *Sử' ký*],   a 130 chapters book covering the history of China up to 90 BC. The author was the great historian Szuma Chien (145-90 BC). In this well-known book were recorded: the actions and statements of the emperors; the names of the kings, noblemen, officials of the *Han* dynasty; the accounts of prominent individuals and families of the pre-imperial period such as Bian Que, Huang Di etc.; the biographies of the main figures of the *Han* dynasty; various subjects such as economy, astronomy etc.

---

hollow pulse [*Kong mai* 乳脉 *Khổng mạch*],   feels like the stem of a green onion: hard outside, empty inside. This type of pulse is seen particularly in cases of massive loss of blood.

---

horizontal inserting [*Heng ci* 横刺 *Hoành thích*],   method indicated where the muscle is thin, particularly on the face and head (Figure 34), e.g. points Gv20 (*Baihui*), St4 (*Dicang*). The needle forms an angle of 15°-20° with the skin surface.

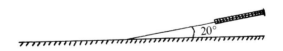

Figure 34: Horizontal inserting

---

horn method [*Jiao fa* 角法 *Dác pháp*],   so-called cupping in ancient times since horn was used for cup (see **cupping therapy**).

Hua Shou (AD 1304-1386) [滑寿 *Hoạt Thọ*],   author of a useful treatise on acupuncture, *The Expounding of the Fourteen Channels* (*Shi*

Si Jing Fa Hui), published in AD 1341 and *The Genuine Meaning of the Difficult Classic* (*Nan Jing Ben Yi*), published in AD 1361.

Hua Tuo (AD 141-212) [华佗 *Hoa Dà*], a famous surgeon who was said to have performed many major operations including abdominal surgery with his oral anaesthetic *Ma Fu Tang* (see **Ma Fu Tang**). According to his biography, he was skilled not only in medicine and surgery but also in acupuncture and moxibustion. He generally used one or two points to achieve the desired effect. He was also said to have used acupuncture to

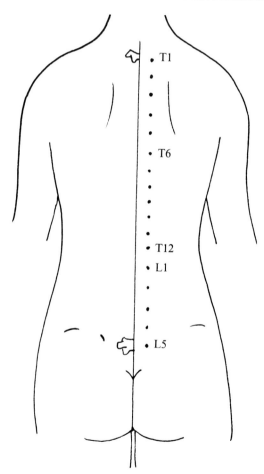

Figure 35: Hua Tuo paravertebral points

treat Tsao Tsao, statesman, strategist of the Three Kingdoms period (AD 220-280) for his chronic headache. Inspired by the movements of five kinds of wild animals, tiger, deer, bear, monkey, bird in flight, he invented a series of physical exercises to cure illnesses and to promote health (see **five animals game method**).

Hua Tuo paravertebral points [*Hua Tuo jia ji* 华佗夹脊 *Hoa Dà giáp tích*], is a group of seventeen pairs of points located about half an inch on either side of the spinous process from the first thoracic vertebra to the fifth lumbar vertebra (Figure 35). It is believed that these points were used as **back-*Shu* points** by the ancient famous physician Hua Tuo. When the functions of certain internal organs are disturbed, the corresponding paravertebral points are tender under pressure. The indications of these paravertebral points are similar to those of the back-*Shu* points (see **associated points**).

Huang Di (2698-2589 BC) [黄帝 *Hoàng Đế*], the third and the most famous of China's five legendary emperors. He was called Huang Di or Yellow Emperor since he ruled by the element Earth whose colour is yellow (Figure 36). He introduced mathematical calculations, invented the agricultural calendar, money, compass, boats, carts, pottery. He made musical instruments and also studied medicine (see **Synopsis of Chinese medical history**).

Huangfu Mi (AD 214-282) [皇甫谧 *Hoàng Phủ Mật*], author of the book *A Classic of Acupuncture and Moxibustion*, the earliest known book of its kind. The treatise consists of twelve rolls and describes clearly and in detail the art of acupuncture and moxibustion (see *Classic of Acupuncture and Moxibustion*).

human inch, see **inch.**

hurried pulse [*Cu mai* 促脉 *Xúc mạch*], is rapid with irregular missing beats, usually seen in cases with excessive **heat,** stagnation of *Qi*, **blood** and **phlegm.**

81

Figure 36: Huang Di or Yellow Emperor (2698-2589 BC) (By courtesy of the University of Hong Kong)

husband-wife relationship [*Fu fu guan xi* 夫妇关系 *Phu phụ quan hệ*],   the left wrist pulse is considered husband pulse and the right pulse wife pulse. Normally, the husband pulse should be slightly stronger than the wife pulse. According to the husband-wife relationship or law, there is correlation between the pulses of the equivalent positions of the right and left wrists (e.g. **heart** and **lung, gall bladder** and **stomach** (Table 6).

Table 6: The relation between the pulses of the equivalent positions of the right and left wrists

	SUPERFICIAL PULSE *Yang Fu* ORGANS	DEEP PULSE *Yin Zang* ORGANS
Left wrist (husband)	Small intestine Gall bladder Urinary bladder	Heart Liver Kidney
Right wrist (wife)	Large intestine Stomach Three heater	Lung Spleen Pericardium

hyperactivity of the stomach [*Wei Huo* 胃火 *Vị hoả*], a condition marked by foul breath, oral ulcer, heartburn, polyphagia, thirst, red tongue with yellow coating, rapid and full pulse. The term '*Wei huo*' literally means stomach **fire**.

I

impairment of body fluid [*Shang jin* 伤津 *Thu'o'ng tân*], specifically refers to the impairment of body fluid of the **lung** and **stomach** with symptoms such as thirst, dry cough, irritability, constipation etc.

impairment of *Yang* [*Shang Yang* 伤阳 *Thu'o'ng Du'o'ng*], may be caused by various factors such as invasion of **cold** or overdosage of cold nature medicines.

impairment of *Yin* [*Shang Yin* 伤阴 *Thu'o'ng Âm*], the most important is the impairment of **liver** and **kidney** *Yin* in advanced cases of febrile diseases.

---

implanting needle [*Liu zhen* 留针 *Mai zhen* 埋针 *Lùù châm Mai châm*], a method of subcutaneous implantation with special needles: *thumbtack type* needle about 0.3cm long with a head like a thumbtack (Figure 42e), suitable for auricular implantation; *grain like type* needle about 1cm long with a head like a grain of wheat suitable for implantation at points and tender spots on the body (Figure 42f). The duration of the implantation depends on the season: *in summer*, due to the perspiration, leave the needles for one or two days only; *in autumn and winter*, the needles can be left for more than two days according to the need. This method of needle implantation is indicated in chronic diseases of the internal organs, chronic and painful diseases.

---

impotence [*Yang wei* 阳痿 *Du'o'ng nuy*], a condition usually caused by damage of the **kidney** *Yang* resulting from sexual over-indulgence or repeated spermatorrhoea. Symptoms are pallor, dizziness, asthenia, weakness of the lumbar region and the knees, frequency. This condition may also be due to injury of *Qi* of the **heart, spleen** and **kidney** resulting from emotional factors such as fright, sorrow.

---

inch [*Cun* 寸 *Thôń*], may refer to: 1. the unit of length (3.33cm or 1.31 in.) used to measure the depth of puncturing; 2. the proportional unit, human inch (*Tong shen cun*) or bone measurement. The width and length of various portions of the human body are divided into definite numbers of equal divisions. Each division represents one *Cun* (Figure 37). The length of the *Cun* is therefore different from patient to patient and from one area to the other; 3. the distance between the two ends of the creases of the interphalangeal joints of the flexed middle finger (Figure 38); 4. one of the three places (inch, bar, cubit or *Cun, Guan, Chi*) where the tip of the physician's index finger rests when taking the patient's pulse (Figure 47). On the left wrist, the inch represents the condition of the pulse of the heart while the inch on the right wrist corresponds to the pulse condition of the lung (see **pulse feeling**).

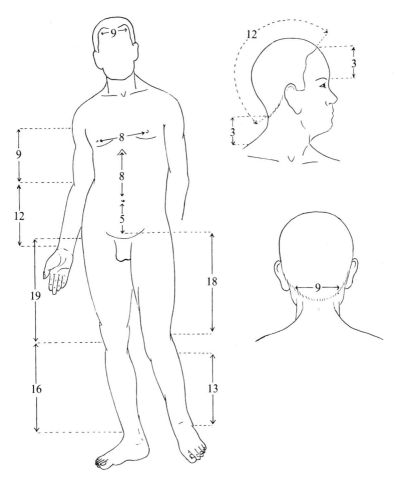

Figure 37: Proportional unit

indirect moxibustion [*Jian jie jiu* 间接灸 *Gián tiếp cứu*], is performed by placing salt or a piece of ginger or garlic between the ignited moxa cone and the skin. The therapeutic effects are different for each material: *ginger*: indicated in vomiting, diarrhoea of cold type, arthralgia, symptoms of *Yang* deficiency; *garlic*: used in early stages of skin infection, poisonous insect bites; *salt*: mainly indicated in emergency cases such as coma, acute abdominal pain. Specially used with acupuncture point Cv8 (*Shenque*).

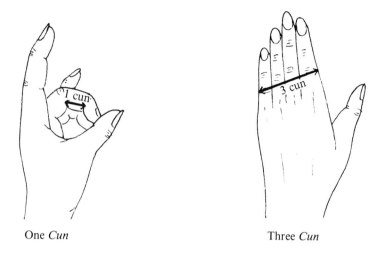

One *Cun*   Three *Cun*

Figure 38: ***Cun* or Chinese inch**

---

inferior spirit, see **animal spirit.**

---

influential points, eight [*Ba hui xue* 八 会 穴 *Bát hội huyệt*], so-called since the *Qi* of the eight tissues meet at these points. Each of the **eight influential points** has an effect on the diseases of certain tissue (Table 7, Figure 39).

Table 7: The eight influential points

TISSUE	INFLUENTIAL POINTS
Zang organs	Liv13 (*Zhangmen*)
Fu organs	Cv12 (*Zhongwan*)
Qi (respiratory system)	Cv17 (*Shanzhong*)
Blood	UB17 (*Geshu*)
Tendon	GB34 (*Yanglingquan*)
Pulse, vessels	Lu9 (*Taiyuan*)
Bone	UB11 (*Dashu*)
Marrow	GB39 (*Xuanzhong*)

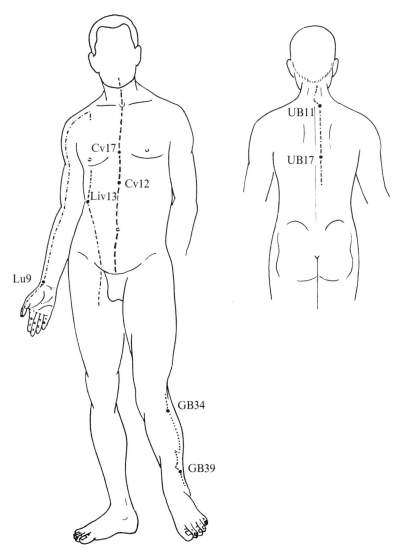

Figure 39: Eight influential points

inspection, ten important points [*Wang zhen shi yao* 望 诊 十要
Vọng chẩn thập yếu], plays an important part in the diagnosis of
diseases in traditional Chinese medicine. To be noted when examining the
patient:

1. *Facial expression* which is the outward manifestation of the vital

activities and may serve as an initial guide to physical or mental disorders.

2. *Appearance*: body build, gait, posture, abnormal movements of the trunk and limbs.

3. *Complexion* which may reveal diseases of some **internal organs**.

4. *Tongue*: disorders of the **internal organs, channels and collaterals,** *Qi*, **blood** and **body fluid** may be manifested in the tongue.

5. *Large bones* which can be affected by serious or chronic diseases.

6. *Teeth* which reflect the states and conditions of the **kidney,** blood circulation, **stomach, spleen.**

7. *Nutritional status.*

8. *Finger prints* which reveal the blood circulation in the superficial capillaries. The diagnosis based on the observation of the index finger veins is particularly helpful in under three-year-old children.

9. *Certain organs* such as the **eyes, mouth, ears** may reveal the states and conditions of the **liver, spleen** and **kidney** respectively.

10. *Hair* on the scalp may reflect the conditions of the **kidney, blood** and *Qi*.

---

intercurrent diseases [*Bing bing* 并病 *He bing* 合病 *Tinh bệnh, Hợp bệnh*], the syndrome of two or more channels appearing at the same time.

---

intermittent pulse [*Dai mai* 代脉 *Đại mạch*], slow with regular missing beats indicating the weak condition of the viscera, it is often seen in cases of **heart** disease.

---

internal organs [*Zang fu* 脏腑 *Tạng phủ*], in traditional Chinese medicine, the physiological functions, the pathological changes and the relationship of an organ with the fundamental substances (*Qi*, blood, body fluid etc.), other organs and other parts of the body are more important than its anatomical structure. The term '*Zang Fu*' in Chinese refers not only to the anatomical entities of the **internal organs** but also to a generalization of the function of the human body. Traditional Chinese medicine divides the internal organs into two groups:

Zang or solid organs: these *Yin* organs are five in number: **heart, liver, spleen, lung** and **kidney** (six if the **pericardium** is included). Their main functions are manufacturing and storing essential substances including *Qi*, **blood** and body fluid.

Fu or hollow organs: the small intestine, **gall bladder, stomach, large intestine, urinary bladder** and **three heater** are known as six *Fu* organs. They are *Yang* organs and their main functions are receiving, digesting foods, absorbing nutrient substances and finally excreting waste materials. The brain and the uterus are considered extraordinary or curious organs (see **extraordinary organs**).

---

interrogation [*Wen zhen* 问 诊 *Vấń chấ̉n*], involves the ten principal questions to ask the patient recommended by Zhang Jie-bin (about AD 1563-1640), a well-known physician in the Ming dynasty.
1. Chills and fever; 2. perspiration; 3. defaecation and urination; 4. pain, headache; 5. appetite; 6. thirst; 7. hearing; 8. feeling in the chest; 9. past history; 10. causes.

J

---

jaundice [*Huang dan* 黄 胆 *Hoàng dản*], according to traditional Chinese medicine, is caused by the dysfunction of the **stomach** and **spleen** resulting in an internal accumulation of **dampness** which affects the normal excretion of bile. Jaundice is of two types: *Yang*, **damp heat** is dominant, symptoms are yellow sclera, skin and urine, fever, abdominal distension, yellow coated tongue; *Yin*, symptoms are lassitude, thick white coated tongue, lustreless yellow.

Jing **(river) points** [*Jing xue* 经 穴 *Kinh huyệt*], one of the **five transporting** (*Shu*) points, indicated in asthma, cough, throat diseases (see **five transporting (*Shu*) points**).

Jing **(well) points** [*Jing xue* 井 穴 *Tỉnh huyệt*], one of the five transporting (*Shu*) points, indicated in mental diseases, stifling sensation in the chest (see **five transporting (*Shu*) points**).

---

joined puncture [*Tou ci* 透 刺 *Thâú thích*] a method of puncturing two or more adjoining points in one insertion of a needle.

K

---

kidneys [*Shen* 肾 *Thận*], one of the five *Zang* organs, play an important part in traditional Chinese medicine. Although the location of the kidneys was well known in traditional Chinese medicine, their function was not very well understood. It was believed that the urine passes from the small intestine into the **urinary bladder** through a hole on the top of the bladder. The ureters were considered the tubes for transporting the semen in males. The main functions of the kidneys are:

1. *Storing Jing Qi* and controlling human reproduction, maturation and development, thus the name 'root of life' given to the kidneys. This is the most important function. The right kidney in man is called 'gate of life' (*Ming men*) and is the place where semen is stored. The sexual potency of men depends upon the kidneys.

2. *Producing* the **marrow,** manufacturing the **blood,** forming the **brain** and ruling the **bones.**

3. *Regulating* the water circulation, maintaining the body fluid balance.

4. *Controlling* the intake of **clean Qi.**

5. *Opening* into the **ear.** Deafness and tinnitus occur when there is deficiency in **kidney Qi.**

6. *Controlling* the will and resolution.

7. *Influencing* the **hair** on the head. The glossiness, colour and growth of the scalp hair depend on the conditions of the **kidneys.** Excessive fright may affect the hair since the kidneys are injured.

8. *Dominating* the **spleen.**

---

kidney Yang [*Shen Yang* 肾 阳 *Thận Du'o'ng*], also called genuine vital function, genuine fire or fire of the gate of life, is believed to be the source of heat energy of the body.

---

kidney *Yin* [*Shen Yin* 肾阴 *Thận Âm*],   also called genuine essence, kidney fluid and is the material basis of vital function of the kidneys.

---

knotted pulse [*Jie mai* 结脉 *Kết mạch*],   slow with irregular missing beats, it is seen in cases of obstruction of *Qi* and **blood** by **cold.**

L

---

large intestine [*Da chang* 大肠 *Dại tru'ò'ng*],   one of the six *Fu* organs, the main functions are to absorb the residue of water coming from the **small intestine** and to transform the rest of the food into faeces. In case of 'descent of *Qi*' the function of the **large intestine** will be disturbed resulting in diarrhoea or constipation.

---

leather pulse [*Ge mai* 革脉 *Cách mạch*],   although large, taut and hard, is as hollow as touching the surface of a drum and indicates the loss of **blood** and semen. '*Ge*' in Chinese means the skin on the top of the drum.

---

lesser *Yang* **syndrome** [*Shaoyang bing* 少阳病 *Thiêú Du'o'ng bệnh*],   which runs between the exterior and interior of the body, is characterized by alternation of chill and fever, sensation of fullness in the chest (see **six channels, diagnosis based on**), bitterness and dryness in the mouth, tight pulse etc.

---

lesser *Yin* **syndrome** [*Shaoyin bing* 少阴病 *Thiêú Âm bệnh*], involves the channel relating to the **heart** and **kidneys.** The main feature is general weakness due to the deficiency of the vital function and vital essence (*Jing*) of these two organs (see **six channels, diagnosis based on**).

Li Shi-zhen or *Bin Hu* (AD 1518-1593) [李时珍 *Lý Thời Trân (Tân*

Hồ)], great physician and naturalist of the Ming dynasty, who spent thirty years in compiling the fifty-two volumes *Materia Medica of Pharmaceutical Botany* (*Ben Cao Gang Mu*), published in AD 1590. His other books include *The Pulse studies of Bin Hu* (*Bin Hu mai xue*) published in AD 1564 and *A Study on the Eight Extra Channels* (*Qi jing mai kao*).

---

lifting and thrusting the needle [*Dao zhen* 搗 针 *Dảo châm*], one of the commonly used tonifying and sedating methods. *Tonifying*: once the needling sensation is felt, lift the needle slowly and gently then thrust it quickly and strongly. *Sedating*: lift the needle rapidly and then thrust it slowly and gently.

---

lips [*Chun* 唇 *Thân*], one of the seven passes — other name, flying door — reflect not only the condition of the **spleen** but also the states of other organs: *pale lips*: deficiency conditions and **cold**; *red lips*: **heat** condition; *dry scorched lips*: **heat** injuring the body fluid; *cracking lips*: **stomach** and **spleen heat**; *trembling lips*: sign of **wind** or weak **spleen**; *swollen lips*: sign of accumulation of **heat** in the **spleen** and **stomach** or food poisoning.

---

listening and smelling [*Wen zhen* 闻 诊 *Văn chân*], is one of the four methods of diagnosis in traditional Chinese medicine. By listening to the speech, the respiration and the cough, the physician may have already some information about the mind, the **heart** and the **lungs** of the patient. Usually the **heat** syndrome of excess type is revealed by an offensive smell and the **cold** syndrome of deficiency type by an insipid odour.

---

liver [*Gan* 肝 *Can*], one of the five *Zang* organs, the main physiological functions are: 1. storing blood; 2. maintaining the free flow of *Qi*; 3. harmonizing the emotions, maintaining the mental balance. Excessive anger may injure the **liver** and conversely, impairment of the **liver** function will cause mental depression, irritability, abdominal distension, jaundice, 'The liver is the dwelling place of the soul or *Hun*'; 4. controlling the **tendons** (including muscles and ligaments); 5. controlling the secretion of **bile**; 6. opening into the **eyes**: symptoms of the **liver** dysfunction may include poor vision, night blindness, nystagmus; 7. generating the **heart** and regulating the **lungs**. The term '*Gan Dan*' (**liver-gall bladder**) means brave, courageous.

---

long pulse [*Chang mai* 长脉 *Tru'ò'ng mạch*], can be felt beyond the inch (*Cun*) and cubit (*Chi*) positions and the stroke is considerably prolonged. In healthy people, the pulse may be long and tardy. However, if the pulse is long and tight, it is a sign of excess.

---

loss of essence of life [*Duo Jing* 夺精 *Doạt tinh*], is manifested when excessive, by pallor, fatigue, palpitation, spontaneous night sweating, weak and thready pulse etc.

---

loss of *Yang* [*Wang Yang* 亡阳 *Vong Du'o'ng*], a condition usually resulting from excessive loss of *Qi* and nutrient fluid, e.g. collapse due to excessive sweating, profuse diarrhoea and vomiting.

---

loss of *Yin* [*Wang Yin* 亡阴 *Vong Âm*], a condition resulting from excessive loss of *Qi* and nutrient fluid due to high fever, excessive sweating and profuse diarrhoea.

---

lower abdomen, see **abdomen.**

---

lower heater, see **three heater.**

---

lungs [*Fei* 肺 *Phê*], one of the five *Zang* organs. The inferior spirit or *Po* dwells in the lungs which are the centre of sorrow. The lungs and the **kidneys** are considered homologous since there is close relationship between the functions of these two organs. The main physiological functions of the lungs are:

1. *dominating Qi* (air) and controlling the respiration, 'The lungs rule *Qi*, inhale Clean Air (*Qing Qi*) and expel polluted *Qi* (*Zhuo Qi*)'; 2. *regulating* the distribution of water in the body; 3. *dominating* the **skin** and **hair**, giving lustre to the skin, growth and shine to the hair, controlling the pores; 4. *opening* into the **nose**: breathing and smelling depend upon the function of the lungs.

M

Ma Fu Tang [麻沸汤 *Ma Phị Thang*], is a kind of oral anaesthetic (mixture of hemp and strong wine) said to have been used by Hua Tuo, the most famous surgeon (AD 141-212) in many major operations including abdominal surgery. '*Ma*' means hemp. '*Fu Tang*' means boiling water.

major collateral of the spleen [*Pi da luo* 脾大络 *Tỳ dại lạc*], one of the fifteen collaterals, emerges from the point Sp21 (*Dabao*), major **connecting** (*Luo*) **point** of the **spleen channel,** and connects with all the connecting (*Luo*) vessels of the main channels. Due to these special connections, in cases of excess (*Shi*) syndrome, pain occurs everywhere in the body and in deficiency (*Xu*) syndrome, the joints become less stiff.

marrow [*Sui* 髓 *Tủy*], in traditional Chinese medicine, refers not only to the bone marrow but also to the spinal cord. The Chinese did not make any distinction between brain, marrow and bone which are always inseparable from the **kidneys** and are dependent on the prenatal and postnatal *Jing*. 'The brain is the Sea of marrow.' The main function of the marrow is to nourish the **bones.** The growth of the bones in children will be affected if the marrow is deficient.

massage, massotherapy [*Tui na liao fa* 推拿疗法 *Thôi nã liệu pháp*], is also a method of treatment in traditional Chinese medicine along with **acupuncture, moxibustion** and herbal medicine. This method has been mentioned in Nei Jing and was very popular during the Tang dynasty (AD 618-907). The traditional massage techniques may include the use of the finger nail, tips of the fingers, knuckles, elbows, toes, knees and heels of the hand for different movements.

meeting points [*Hui xue* 会穴 *Hội huyệt*], are intersection points of two or more channels, mostly located on the head, face, trunk and are indicated in diseases relating to several channels. Among the special meeting points, the most important are those of the **governing** (*Du*) and **conception**

(*Ren*) **vessels.** The point Cv1 (*Huiyin*) is the meeting point of all the *Yin* channels and is prescribed in irregular menstruation, urinary retention, enuresis, spermatorrhea, mental disorders. The point hundred meetings (*Baihui*) or Gv20 is the crossing point of the three leg *Yang* and the **governing** (*Du*) **vessel.** It is prescribed in mental diseases, apoplexy, prolapse of the rectum, blurring of vision.

---

meridian, see **channel.**

---

metal [*Jin* 金 *Kim*], one of the **five phases** symbolizing the **lung.** According to the theory of Five Phases, metal (lung) promotes water (kidney), acts on wood (liver) and counteracts fire (heart) (see **five phases**).

---

midday-midnight relationship [*Zheng wu ye ban guan xi* 正午夜半关系 *Chính ngọ dạ bán quan hệ*], *Qi* flows through various organs in a definite order and it is believed that each of the twelve organs has a two-hour period during which its activity is maximal and thus is more responsive to the treatment (Figure 40). The needling should be carried out at the appropriate time of the day to obtain the best result (e.g. the liver should be treated between 1 and 3 a.m. to have the optimum result). This law can also be used in diagnosis (e.g. the colicky pain at midnight could be caused either by the **gall bladder** or the **heart**).

---

middle heater, see **three heater.**

---

middle part of the stomach cavity [*Zhong wan* 中脘 *Trung quản*], is also the name of the acupuncture point Cv12 used in gastric pain, abdominal distension, vomiting, diarrhoea. The Chinese term refers to the middle part of the stomach cavity.

---

mother-child relationship [*Mu zi guan xi* 母子关系 *Mâu tử quan hệ*], *Qi* flows through the twelve main channels in a definite sequence. The cycle starts from the **lung channel** and after arriving at the last channel which is the **liver channel,** the cycle begins again with the **lung channel** (Figure 40). According to the mother-child relationship or law, a channel

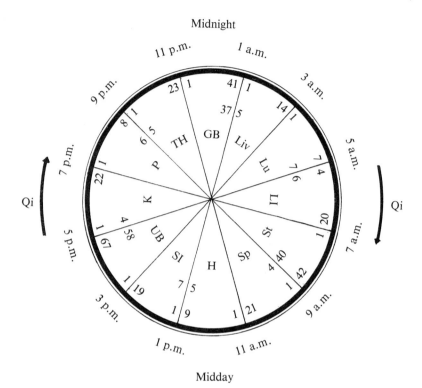

Midnight

Figure 40: Midday-midnight relationship and the order of circulation of *Qi* and blood in the twelve regular channels.

The figures near the circumference represent the entry and exit points and those near the centre are the connecting (*Luo*) points.

that precedes another is its 'mother' and one that immediately follows it is its 'child' (e.g. the **small intestine channel** is the 'mother' of the **urinary bladder channel** and at the same time the 'child' of the **heart channel**. The 'mother' has a tonifying effect and is prescribed in deficiency syndrome. The 'child' has a sedating effect and is indicated in excess syndrome. 'Reinforce the mother for deficiency (*Xu*) syndrome, Reduce the child for excess (*Shi*) syndrome.' This mother-child relationship can apply to the law of five phases. For example in cases of deficiency of the **lung,** the **spleen** (mother) should be tonified; in excess syndrome of the **lung,** the **kidney** (child) should be sedated.

ACUPUNCTURE & MOXIBUSTION

mouth [*Kou* 口 *Khâù*], can reflect the conditions of some internal organs. The **spleen** and the **mouth** are closely related in their functions of receiving, transporting and digesting food. 'The spleen opens into the mouth.' Excessive salivation is the manifestation of a weak spleen injured by **dampness** and **heat** in the stomach. Drooping of the corner of the mouth as in hemiplegia is a sign of being attacked by **evil wind.** Impossibility of closing the mouth is seen in case of excessive deficiency.

moving pulse [*Dong mai* 动脉 *Dộng mạch*], slippery, quick and jerky is seen in cases of intense fright, pain, fever or in pregnant women.

moxa [*Ai* 艾 *Ngải*], from the Japanese word Mokusa or Mogusa which means burning herb, is the dried leaf of artimesia vulgaris or mugwort used in **moxibustion.** The material used is mainly moxa wool which is made of dry, finely ground moxa. It can be used either as small cones of different sizes or as sticks (Figure 41a.b.).

moxibustion [*Jiu* 灸 *Cu'ú'*], is the method of treatment and prevention of diseases by applying heat to points or certain selected locations of the body with burning moxa wool in the form of sticks or cones. It has the properties of warming and removing obstruction of the **channels,** eliminating **cold** and **dampness** (Figure 41).

The methods of application of moxa can be summarized as follows:

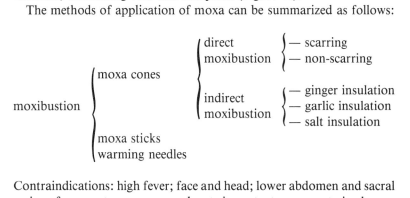

Contraindications: high fever; face and head; lower abdomen and sacral region of pregnant women; areas close to important organs, arteries, bones.

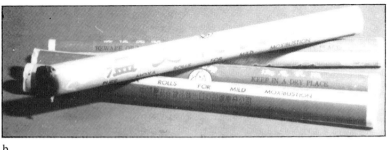

b

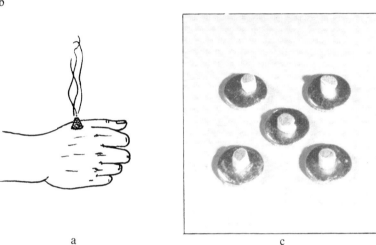

a   c

Figure 41: (a) Moxa cone; (b) moxa sticks; (c) mini moxa.

moxibustion with warm needles [*Wen zhen jiu* 温 针 灸 *Ôn châm cu'ú'*], one of the three methods of application of moxibustion. A piece of moxa wool is wrapped around the handle of the inserted needle and burned (Figure 41c). This method is particularly indicated in diseases such as arthralgia due to **cold** and **dampness.**

---

mugwort, see **artimesia vulgaris.**

---

muscle channels [*Jin jing* 筋 经 *Cân kinh*], so-called since these channels — twelve in all — are involved in diseases affecting muscles and joints and have no connection with the internal organs although they get their names from the nearest main channels. They start from the extremities of the upper and lower limbs and end at the head, face or trunk and some areas of the skin where the collaterals are found.

N

nails [*Jia* 甲 *Giáp*], since the liver is manifested in the nails, thin and pale ones are a sign of **liver** dysfunction; pink and moist nails are seen in cases of excessive **liver blood.**

needle [*Zhen* 针 *Châm*], according to the *Historical Records* by Szuma Chien (145-90 BC), in paleolithic age, the earliest needles were made of stone and were called *Bian shi* (stone piercer), *Chan shi* (stone borer), *Zhen shi* (stone needle). By neolithic times, the needles were made of bone, bamboo and later they were made of gold, silver, copper and other metals. Nei Jing mentioned nine kinds of needles used in acupuncture. In 1968, nine puncturing needles (four gold and five silver) were found in the tombs of Liu Sheng and his wife in Hopei province. The most commonly used needles today are made of high quality stainless steel (Figure 42c). There has been controversy about the metal being used. The yellow metals (gold, copper) are believed to have a *Yang* or stimulating power and the white metals (silver, chrome) a *Yin* or sedating power. A good needle should be strong and flexible, the body round and smooth, the tip shaped like a pine needle. The size and length of the needles most commonly used are as follows:

Length							
inch	0.5	1	1.5	2	2.5	3	4	5
mm	12.7	25.4	38.1	50.8	63.5	76.2	101.6	127

Calibre			
gauge	26	28	30	32
diameter mm	0.46	0.38	0.32	0.26

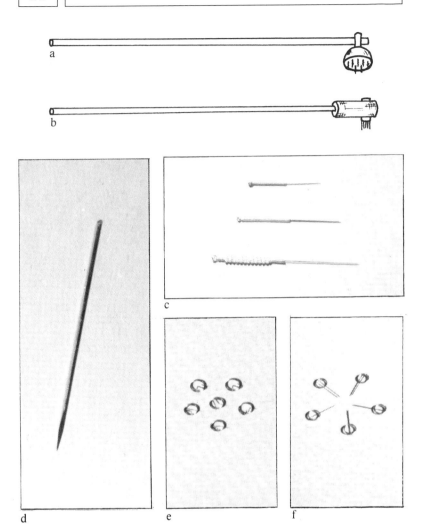

(a) seven-star needle; (b) plum blossom needle; (c) filiform needles; (d) three-edge needle; (e) thumbtack type embedding needles; (f) grain-like type embedding needles.

Figure 42: Different types of needles

---

needles, nine [*Jiu zhen* 九針 *Cu'ů' châm*], mentioned in Nei Jing (Figure 43):

    1. *Arrow headed* needle: one *Cun*, six *Fen* long (see **Chinese weights**

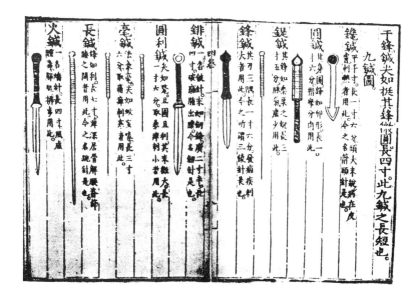

Figure 43: The nine kinds of acupuncture needles from *The Compendium of Acupuncture and Moxibustion* (*Zhen Jiu Da Cheng*, AD 1601).

and measures) for superficial pricking.

   2. *Round* needle: one *Cun*, six *Fen* long for massaging.

   3. *Blunt* needle: three *Cun*, five *Fen* long for knocking or pressing.

   4. *Sharp* three-edged needle: one *Cun*, six *Fen* long for venous pricking.

   5. *Sword like* needle: four *Cun* long, one point five *Cun* large for evacuating pus.

   6. *Sharp round* needle: one *Cun*, six *Fen* long for rapid pricking.

   7. *Filiform* needle: three *Cun*, six *Fen* long, the most commonly used.

   8. *Long* needle: seven *Cun* long for deep puncture.

   9. *Large* needle: four *Cun* long for arthritis or arthralgia.

Nei Jing, Huang Di Nei Jing [内经，黄帝内经 *Nội kinh, Hoàng Đế Nội Kinh*], the *Internal Classic* or *Canon of Medicine* is the oldest and the greatest medical book extant in China with its authorship ascribed to Huang Di, the third of five emperors of the legendary period. In fact, the work was a product of various unknown authors in the Warring States Period (475-221 BC). The book consists of two parts: *Su Wen* or

Plain Questions and *Ling Shu* or Miraculous Pivot, also known as Canon of Acupuncture. The first and important part takes the form of a dialogue between Huang Di and his minister Qi Bo regarding the basic concepts of Chinese medicine (two opposing forces of *Yin* and *Yang*, Tao concept, theory of **five phases**) which remain the dominating theory of traditional Chinese medicine to the present day.

nocturnal emission [*Meng yi* 梦 遗 *Mộng di*], caused by anxiety, sexual over-indulgence, leading to weakness of the **kidney** and excess of **fire** in the heart. Symptoms are 'morning after' dizziness, palpitation, listlessness, lassitude.

non exo-endogenous pathogenic factors [*Bu nei bu wai yin* 不 内 不 外 因 *Bất nội bất ngoại nhân*], are not related either to the external or internal influences but to: *diet*: intemperance in eating, drinking; *sexual activity*: over-indulgence will damage the kidney *Jing*; *physical activity*: exhaustion, fatigue, lack of physical exertion; *miscellaneous factors*: burns, insect or animal stings and bites, cuts, contusion etc.

normal transmission [*Shun zhuan* 顺 传 *Thuận truyền*], refers to the normal passing of a disease from one channel to another such as from greater (*Tai*) *Yang* to sunlight (*Ming*) *Yang* or lesser (*Shao*) *Yang* or from a *Yang* channel to a *Yin* channel.

nose [*Bi* 鼻 *Ty*], may reflect the states of certain internal organs: the inspiratory dilatation of the *alae nasi* is a sign of **heat** in the lungs. 'The lungs open into the nose.' *Red and swollen* nose indicates stomach and spleen dampness. *White* nose is a sign of deficient *Qi*. Stagnation of food in the intestine is revealed by a *white* and shiny nose.

nourishing *Qi*, see *Qi*.

numbness, see *Bi* **syndrome**.

O

oblique inserting [*Xie ci* 斜刺 *Tà thích*], the needle forms an angle about 45° with the skin surface, particularly indicated in areas where the muscle is thin or close to important viscera (Figure 44).

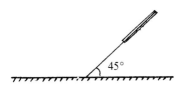

Figure 44: Oblique inserting

obstruction and rejection [*Guan ge* 关格 *Quan cách*], may refer to: 1. vomiting and constipation, urinary retention; 2. urinary retention and diarrhoea; 3. a kind of strong pulse indicating dissociation of *Yin* and *Yang*.

oedema [*Shui zhong* 水肿 *Thủy thũng*], other name *shui Qi* (water *Qi*), involves the overflow of excess fluid in the body due to obstruction of the water passages in the **three heater,** caused by invasion of the **lung** by **wind** and **cold** or by deficiency of *Yang* in the **spleen** and **kidney.** Oedema is of two types: *excess* (*Shi*), the onset is abrupt, oedema starts on the face, head or lower limbs; *deficiency (Xu)*, after an insidious onset, oedema first appears on the feet, eyelids then spreads all over the entire body (anasarca).

openings, body [*Miao qiao* 苗窍 *Miêu khiêú*], refers to the openings of the **internal organs.** The **nose, mouth, eye, ear, tongue** are the openings of the **lung, spleen, liver, kidney** and **heart** respectively. The term *Qiao* is sometimes referred to a large cavity such as the thoracic cavity, the abdominal cavity.

openings, lower [*Xia qiao* 下窍 *Hạ khiêú*], refer to the urethral opening and the **anus.**

---

openings, nine [*Jiu qiao* 九窍 *Cu'ủ' khiêú*], refer to seven major body openings namely: **eyes, ears, nostrils, mouth** and two lower openings: urethral opening and **anus.** In diagnosis, the seven major openings are among the usual points of observation.

---

outer appearance of the viscera [*Xiang* 象 *Tu'ọ'ng*], may be reflected in the patient's appearance. The **heart** stores, harbours the **spirit,** influences the **face.** The **lungs** house the **animal spirit** or inferior **soul,** dominate the **skin** and **hair.** The **kidneys** influence the **hair** on the head and dominate the **bones.** The **liver** houses the **soul,** influences the **nails,** controls the **tendons** and muscles. The **stomach, large intestine, small intestine, urinary bladder** and **three heater** influence the **lips,** flesh and muscles.

P

---

pathogenic factors, diagnosis based on [*Bing yin bian zheng* 病因辨证 *Bệnh nhân biện chú'ng*], are divided into three groups:

1. *Six exogenous factors*: **wind, cold, summer heat, dampness, dryness, heat (fire, mild heat).** Diseases caused by these six pathogenic factors are called exogenous diseases (see appropriate heading for details).

2. *Seven emotional factors*: diseases caused by seven emotional factors joy, anger, meditation, anxiety, fear, grief, fright, usually show dysfunction of *Zang Fu* organs and disturbance in *Qi and* **blood** circulation.

3. *Miscellaneous pathogenic factors*: diet: irregular food intake affecting the stomach and spleen; sexual over-indulgence damaging the kidney *Jing*; overstrain and stress affecting the circulation of *Qi* and blood; miscellaneous factors such as burns, trauma, insect or animal stings and bites, parasites etc.

---

pecking pulse [*Que hui mai* 雀 喙 脉 *Tu'ó'c dế mach*],   arrhythmic and quick, resembles the pecking of a bird. It is one of the seven kinds of pulse indicating impending death.

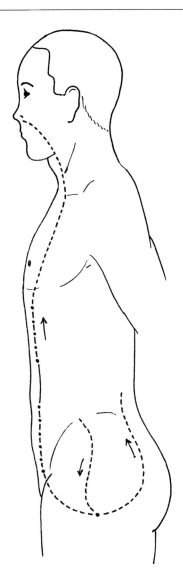

Figure 45: The penetrating (*Chong*) channel

P | ACUPUNCTURE & MOXIBUSTION

penetrating (*Chong*) channel [*Chong mai* 沖脈 *Xung mạch*],
so-called since this channel communicates with all the main channels: 'Sea
of the twelve channels'. It is one of the eight extra channels and, like the
conception vessel, originates in the **uterus** (Figure 45). Spasm and
abdominal pain are pathological manifestations of this extra channel.
'Chong' means vital, penetrating.

---

pericardium [*Xin bao* 心包 *Xiao xin*, 小心, *Tâm bào, Tiê'u tâm*],
also called small heart or cardia minor (*Xiao xin*), and in some texts, organ
of circulation. Although regarded only as an attachment to the **heart,** for
clinical purposes the pericardium is considered the sixth *Yin* organ and
has a separate channel in acupuncture. This pericardium channel has been
translated into English by some as *circulation sex* and into French as
'*Méridien du Maître du coeur*' or '*Méridien du vaisseau sexualité*'.

---

perineum [*Hui Yin* 会阴 *Hội Âm*], also the name of the acupuncture
point Cv1 located in its centre where all the *Yin* channels meet. The term
'*Hui Yin*' literally means meeting of *Yin*. It is indicated in prurit vulvae,
irregular menstruation, urinary retention, seminal emission, mental
disorder, enuresis.

---

perpendicular inserting [*Zhi ci* 直刺 *Trụ'c thích*], as the name
suggests, is a method of inserting the needle perpendicularly to the skin
surface (Figure 46).

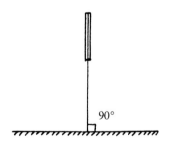

90°

Figure 46: Perpendicular inserting

perverse *Qi,* **evil** *Qi* [*Li Qi* 疠 气 *Lệ khí*], see **pestilential factor.**

---

pestilential factor [*Yi Qi* 疫 气 *Dịch khí*], other names include perverse *Qi* (*Li Qi*), poison *Qi* (*Du Qi*), demon *Qi* (*Xie Qi*). Besides the six **exogenous pathogenic factors,** there is the pestilential factor which causes epidemic diseases. It is similar to the pathogenic **heat** in nature but more dangerous. Pestilential diseases are often fatal and simultaneously affect many people in an area.

---

phlegm [*Tan* 痰 *Dàm*], a term referring to: 1. the pathologic secretions of the diseased respiratory apparatus; 2. the pathologic mucous discharge of any organ which may act as a pathogenic factor.

Phlegm is different from **saliva** (*Xian*) which is translucent, colourless, thin, useful. Phlegm is stringy, thick, greyish, yellowish or greenish, useless, dangerous, usually produced by the respiratory tract and seen in case of ill health. According to traditional Chinese medicine, the disorder of the **lungs, spleen** and **kidneys** will disturb the normal distribution of the body fluid resulting in the formation of phlegm which is condensed body fluid. Symptoms and signs caused by phlegm depend on the place where the secretion is found: **lungs:** cough, asthma, excessive expectoration of sputum; **heart:** rattle in the throat, coma; **channels and collaterals:** numbness of the limbs or hemiplegia if the channels and collaterals are blocked by phlegm.

---

plum blossom acupuncture [*Mei hua zhen* 梅花针 *Mai hoa châm*], also called cutaneous acupuncture (*Pi fu zhen*) or superficial tapping method, is an ancient method of treatment existing more than a thousand years in China. The term plum blossom refers to the five needles bound together to tap lightly at the surface skin of the affected area or along certain lines (Figure 42b).

---

points, acupuncture [*Xue wei* 穴位 *Huyệt vị*], are specific sites through which the *Qi* of the internal organs and channels is carried to the body surface. In cases of disease, the application of moxibustion and/or acupuncture at the appropriate points on the body surface will regulate the flow of *Qi* and **blood** in the channels. Classically, there are 361 regular points. However if all the extraordinary points and those used in ear acupuncture are included, the total number of acupuncture points will rise to 2000. In practice, about 150 points only are necessary for general use.

There are three categories of points:

1. *Points of the fourteen channels,* are 361 in number, recognized by the classical theory. The points of the twelve regular channels, in pairs, are distributed symmetrically on the left and right sides of the body. The points of the two extra channels, **conception** and **governing vessels,** are single and aligned on the anterior and posterior midlines respectively.

2. *Extraordinary or new points,* discovered in the course of practice, these points have definite locations but are not listed in the system of the fourteen channels.

3. *Ah Shi (ah yes) points,* these tender points are present in certain diseases but have neither definite locations nor specific names.

Each acupuncture point has a definite therapeutic indication. They are mostly used in combination. A typical treatment usually needs from five to fifteen needle insertions. The depth of the insertion depends on the particular points.

---

point injection therapy [*Shu zhen liao fa* 水针疗法 *Thủy châm liệu pháp*], is the combination of Chinese and Western methods of treatment: distilled water or drugs in small doses are injected into the selected points or tender spots. This method of therapy is said to be economical and effective in a short period of time.

---

poison *Qi,* see **pestilential factor.**

---

pollution [*Zhuo* 浊 *Trọc*], 'Zhuo' means pollution, impurity, dirtiness. The function of certain organs in the body is said to be dirty when it is related to the excretion or secretion (e.g. function of the **kidneys**). Some organs such as the **small intestine** have both the clean function of absorption and the dirty function of excretion. The term 'Zhuo Qi' or polluted *Qi* refers either to the impure part of the essence of food or the expired waste gas and the flatus.

---

pore [*Xuan fu* 玄府 *Huyền phủ*], relates to the term '*Xuan fu*' meaning mysterious or profound (*Xuan*) site (*Fu*). Other names include gas portal (*Qi men*), devil's portal (*Gui men*). Sweat is the ultimate transformation of the **lung** air (*Fei Qi*) and is exuded as an end product.

Prescriptions Worth a Thousand Gold [*Qian jin yao fang* 千金要方 *Thiên kim yêu phu'o'ng*], other name: *Thousand Gold Remedies for Emergencies* (*Bei ji qian jin yao fang*) — compiled by Sun Si-miao (AD 581-682) in AD 652, the treatise deals with various specialities such as herbals, obstetrics, paediatrics, pulse feeling, acupuncture, moxibustion etc.

---

prickled tongue surface [*Mang ci she* 芒刺舌 *Mang thích thiệt*], results from proliferation and hypertrophy of taste buds, indicating hyperactivity of pathogenic **heat** in the **internal organs.**

---

prompt prick [*Dian ci* 点刺 *Diểm thích*], a fast pricking method used in acupuncture.

---

proportional unit, see **inch.**

---

pubis [*Heng gu* 横骨 *Hoành cốt*], the term '*heng gu*' means transverse bone and refers to: the *os pubis*; the *acupuncture point K11*, located on the superior border of symphysis pubis, 0.5 *Cun* lateral to Cv2 and indicated in pain in the external genitalia, spermatorrhea, impotence. Other name: curved bone (*Qu gu*).

Pulse Classic [*Mai jing* 脉经 *Mạch kinh*], first comprehensive book on sphygmology now extant in China, written by Wang Xi (about AD 210-285).

---

pulse feeling [*Qie mai* 切脉 *Thiết mạch*], the art of feeling the patient's pulse by the physician with the index, middle and ring fingers. It constitutes the very important basis of traditional Chinese diagnosis. The Chinese and Vietnamese usually speak of going to the physician, be he a traditional or western-style physician, as 'going to the physician for the pulse feeling'. The private office of the physician is commonly called the 'pulse office'. The three fingers of the physician (index, middle and ring fingers) are placed above the wrist at the site of the radial artery (*Cunkou*) as shown on Figure 47. The pulse can therefore be felt in three positions: the first position, next to the hand and corresponding to the physician's index finger, is called inch or *Cun*; the second position, next to the first position and corresponding to the middle finger, is called bar or *Guan*; the third position, corresponding to the ring finger, is named cubit or *Chi*. The pulse is felt at two levels of pressure: superficial and deep. A normal pulse should be of regular rhythm, even and forceful with four to five beats per physician's breath. There are six pulses at each wrist: three superficial and three deep. Each pair superficial and deep has a definite place. The superficial pulses relate to *Yang* and the deep pulses to *Yin*. There is a relationship between the pulse positions and the internal organs (Table 8, Figure 47).

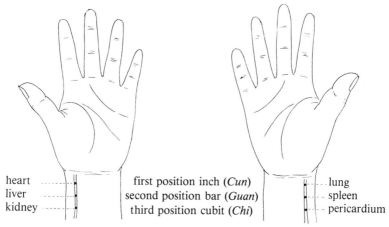

heart ------
liver ------
kidney ------

first position inch (*Cun*)
second position bar (*Guan*)
third position cubit (*Chi*)

lung
spleen
pericardium

Figure 47: The three positions for feeling pulse

pulse, twenty-eight types [*Er shi ba mai* 二十八脉 *Nhị thập bát mạch*], are usually referred to in modern texts as follows:

1. Big (*Da*)	7. Flooding (*Hong*)	13. Hurried (*Cu*)
2. Confined (*Lao*)	8. Full (*Shi*)	14. Intermittent (*Dai*)
3. Deep (*Chen*)	9. Hard, tight (*Jin*)	15. Knotted (*Jie*)
4. Empty (*Xu*)	10. Hesitant, choppy (*Se*)	16. Leather (*Ge*)
5. Fine (*Wei*)	11. Hidden (*Fu*)	17. Long (*Chang*)
6. Floating (*Fu*)	12. Hollow (*Kong*)	18. Moving (*Dong*)

19. Rapid (*Shu*)
20. Scattered (*San*)
21. Short (*Duan*)
22. Slippery (*Hua*)

23. Slow (*Chi*)
24. Soggy (*Ru*)
25. Tardy (*Huan*)

26. Thready (*Xi*)
27. Weak (*Ruo*)
28. Wiry (*Xian*)

However the number of types of pulse varies according to different sources: twenty after Nei Jing, twenty-four according to Wang Xi in his *Pulse Classic* and twenty-eight after Li Zhong-li, author of the *Origin of Materia Medica*.

Table 8: The relationship between pulse positions and internal organs

	POSITIONS	INTERNAL ORGANS	
		SUPERFICIAL PULSE *Yang*	DEEP PULSE *Yin*
Left	Inch (*Cun*) Bar (*Guan*) Cubit (*Chi*)	Small intestine Gall bladder Urinary bladder	Heart Liver Kidney
Right	Inch (*Cun*) Bar (*Guan*) Cubit (*Chi*)	Large intestine Stomach Three heater	Lung Spleen Pericardium

purple complexion [*Qing se* 青色 *Thanh sắc*], is caused by stagnation or obstruction of *Qi* and **blood** indicating presence of **cold**, pain, blood stasis, convulsions.

purple tongue [*Qing zi se she* 青紫色舌 *Thanh tử sắc thiệt*], results from stagnation of **blood.**

pylorus [*You men* 幽门 *U môn*], term literally meaning dim or remote gate, is considered one of the seven passes of the alimentary tract. It is also the name of the acupuncture point K21, indicated in abdominal pain and vomiting.

Q

Qi [气 *Khí*], often spelled *Ch'i* or *Ki* in Japanese, is one of the fundamental concepts of Chinese thought. It is difficult to have an accurate translation of this term into Western languages. Besides the ordinary meaning of air, *Qi* is an invisible force which gives life to all living matter. Thanks to it, we can live, breathe, think etc. Thus, *Qi* could be understood as a life or vital energy. According to traditional Chinese medicine, this invisible *Qi* or vital energy circulates along a system of conduits called channels or meridians in the body. The force, flow and distribution of *Qi* in the body depend on the balance of *Yin* and *Yang*. Normal *Qi* or upright (*Zheng*) or true (*Zhen*) *Qi* is *Qi* without any specific function and is formed by: 1. source or congenital (*Yuan*) *Qi* or *Qi* of the **kidney**, inherited from parents and related to the function of reproduction; 2. grain (*Gu*) *Qi* from essence of food; 3. natural air (*Kong*) *Qi* from atmospheric air. Once formed, the normal *Qi* will be differentiated into different types with specific functions. Among them are five important types, namely: 1. *internal organs (Zang Fu) Qi*, related to a specific organ, e.g. **kidney** *Qi*, **heart** *Qi*, **lung** *Qi* etc.; 2. *channels and collaterals (Jing luo) Qi*, normal *Qi* circulating in a network of channels and collaterals to different organs and parts of the body; 3. *nourishing (Ying) Qi*, essential factor moving with the blood through the vessels to nourish the body; 4. *defensive (Wei) Qi*, circulates outside the vessels, defending the body against the **exogenous pathogenic factors**; 5. *ancestral (Zong) Qi*, formed in the chest to nourish the **heart** and **lungs** and to promote their functions.

The symptom complexes of disharmonies of *Qi* depend on the types of disharmonies, e.g. deficient, collapsed, stagnant, rebellious *Qi* etc. and the affected organs or channels.

Qi Bo [歧伯 *Kỳ Bá*], Huang Di's minister who, in *Nei Jing*, discussed with the emperor the basic theories of traditional Chinese medicine. The Chinese medical profession was sometimes called 'the art of Qi Huang' (*Qi Huang Zhi Shu*).

Qiao **channels**, see *Yang* **heel channels** and *Yin* **head channels**.

Qin Yue-ren (about 225 BC) [秦 越 人 *Tân Việt Nhân*], is believed to have been the famous physician, Bian Que. The authorship of the *Difficult Classic* (*Nan Jing*) has been ascribed to him.

R

radial pulse site [*Cun kou* 寸口 *Qi kou* 气口 *Thốn khẩu, Khí khẩu*], literally meaning inch mouth (*Cun kou*) or *Qi* mouth (*Qi kou*), is the place on the wrist over the radial artery where the pulse is felt.

rapid pulse [*Shuo mai* 数脉 *Sô' mạch*], has more than five beats per physician's breath and indicating **heat.**

rebellious *Qi* [*Qi ni* 气逆 *Khí nghịch*], moves in the wrong direction, e.g. vomiting and nausea caused by the stomach *Qi* which moves upward instead of downward as normally.

rectum, prolapse [*Tuo gang* 脱肛 *Thoát giang*], like the prolapse of the uterus, is caused by the collapsed *Qi*.

reducing method [*Xie fa* 泻法 *Tả pháp*], to have a reducing effect, the needle can be manipulated as follows: 1. lift the needle forcefully and quickly then thrust it gently and slowly; 2. rotate the needle back and forth with large amplitude continuously and quickly.

reflexology [*Fan she liao fa* 反射疗法 *Phản xạ liệu pháp*], also called zone therapy, is an ancient method of diagnosis and treatment in which the soles of the feet are massaged deeply. The area to be massaged corresponds to the affected organ (Figures 48, 49). It is believed that this method of treatment evolved at the same time as acupuncture in China.

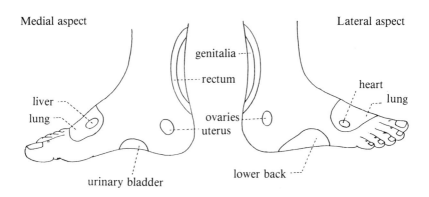

Figure 48: Representation on the feet of some internal organs (medial and lateral aspects)

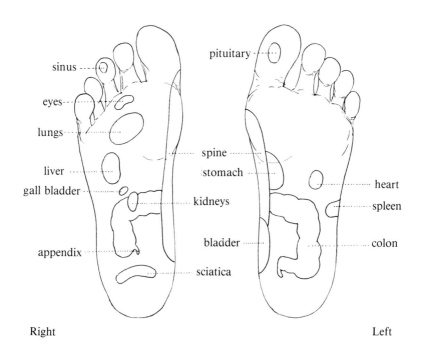

Figure 49: Representation on the feet of some internal organs (plantar aspects)

Reflexology has only been known in the West early this century thanks to the works of W. H. Fitzgerald and E. D. Ingham in the United States.

reinforcing method [*Bu fa* 补法 *Bô' pháp*], to have a reinforcing effect, the needle can be manipulated as follows: 1. once the needle sensation is felt, lift the needle gently and slowly then thrust it strongly and quickly; 2. rotate the needle back and forth with small amplitude continuously and slowly.

ren channel, see **conception vessel.**

rheumatic diseases [*Feng bi* 风痹 *Feng shi* 风湿 *Phong tê, Phong thấp*], are conditions caused by **wind** and **cold** (*Feng Bi*) or by **wind** and **dampness** (*Feng Shi*) (see **Bi syndrome**).

rotating method [*Nian zhen* 捻针 *Niệm châm*], a method of manipulating the needle for reinforcing or reducing effects (see **reducing method** and **reinforcing method**).

Ryodoraku therapy, autonomous nerve regulatory therapy, is an electrostimulating treatment based on the Ryodoraku theory developed by Y. Nakatani in Japan in 1950. According to this concept, in the majority of cases, diseases are caused by the disturbance of the function of the autonomic nerves. Thus the treatment is to try to regulate the disturbed function of the autonomic nervous system by stimulating the acupuncture points with a small electrical stimulator (see **electro-acupuncture**).

S

saliva [*Xian* 涎 *Diên*], a translucent, colourless, thinnish liquid, is a useful secretion since it moistens the mouth, cleanses the tongue, makes speech easier. By moistening the food in the mouth, it dissolves particles to facilitate the chemical action. Saliva should be distinguished from **phlegm** which is useless and pathological.

scalp acupuncture [*Tou zhen liao fa* 头 针 疗 法 *Thủ châm liệu pháp*], a method developed recently (1970) in China, is based on

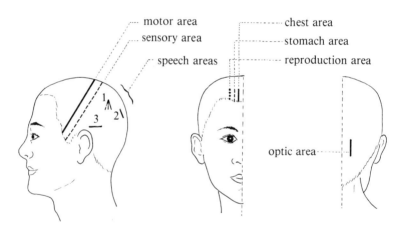

Figure 50: Scalp areas

elementary functional neuro-anatomy. Since all the scalp points are representations of the underlying functional areas of the **brain** (Figure 50), scalp acupuncture is particularly prescribed in diseases such as stroke or severe head injuries causing brain damage.

scattered pulse [*San mai* 散 脉 *Tản mạch*], diffuses on light touch and is not perceptible on hard pressure, seen in critical conditions.

---

scraping and pinching [*Gua sha* 刮 痧 *Quát sa*], a very popular method of treatment of common diseases such as headache, common cold, acute gastroenteritis: 1. the patient's neck, chest, back are scraped with a coin, a comb or a spoon moistened with vegetable oil or balm. If purpura-like marks are produced, the patient has common cold and the toxin is thus removed; 2. the skin between the eyebrows or neck is pinched with the thumb and index finger; petechiae are observed in case of common cold.

---

sea of blood [*Xue hai* 血 海 *Huyết hải*], refers to:

1. the **penetrating (*Chong*) channel** which is considered 'the sea of the twelve channels'.

2. the **liver,** regarded as the main reservoir of **blood** in the body.

3. the acupuncture point Sp10 which is indicated in irregular menstruation, dysmenorrhea, amenorrhea, uterine bleeding. ·

---

sea of marrow [*Sui hai* 髓 海 *Tủy hải*], refers to the **brain**: 'The brain is the sea of marrow' (see **brain** and **marrow**).

---

sea of pollution [*Zhuo hai* 浊海 *Trọc hải*], is formed by five centres of collection and elimination of waste materials namely:

1. **lungs:** waste gas;
2. **kidneys:** broken down nitrogens;
3. **urinary bladder:** fluid wastes, products of the kidneys;
4. **large intestine:** solid and semi-solid wastes;
5. **skin:** sweat.

---

sea of *Qi* [*Qi hai* 气海 *Khí hải*], refers to the area of the breast between the nipples, around the point Cv17 (*Shan zhong*) and having close relation with the heart and lungs. Some hold there are the upper sea of *Qi* around Cv17 and the lower sea of *Qi* corresponding to the point Cv6 (*Qi hai*).

---

sea of water and grains [*Shui gu zhi hai* 水谷之海 Thủy cốc chi hải],   refers to the **stomach**(see **granary**).

---

sedating child,   see **mother-child relationship.**

---

sedation points [*Xie xue* 泻 穴 *Tả huyệt*],   of a channel is the 'child' point of its own phase e.g. the **kidney** belongs to water, the following phase or 'child' is wood, the sedation point is therefore K1 (Table 9).

Table 9: The 'Mother' and 'Child' Points

CHANNELS	'MOTHER' POINTS (TONIFICATION)	'CHILD' POINTS (SEDATION)
Lung	Lu9 (*Taiyuan*)	Lu5 (*Chize*)
Large intestine	LI11 (*Quchi*)	LI2 (*Erjian*)
Stomach	St41 (*Jiexi*)	St45 (*Lidui*)
Spleen	Sp2 (*Dadu*)	Sp5 (*Shangqiu*)
Heart	H9 (*Shaochong*)	H7 (*Shenmen*)
Small intestine	SI3 (*Houxi*)	SI8 (*Xiaohai*)
Urinary bladder	UB67 (*Zhiyin*)	UB65 (*Shugu*)
Kidney	K7 (*Fuliu*)	K1 (*Yongquan*)
Pericardium	P9 (*Zhongchong*)	P7 (*Daling*)
Three heater	TH3 (*Hand-Zhongzhu*)	TH10 (*Tianjing*)
Gall Bladder	GB43 (*Xiazi*)	GB38 (*Yangfu*)
Liver	Liv8 (*Ququan*)	Liv2 (*Xinjian*)

---

seven emotions [*Qi qing* 七 情 *Thất tình*],   are:
1. happiness, joy (*Xi*);
2. anger (*Nu*);
3. anxiety (*You*);
4. sorrow, meditation (*Si*);
5. fear (*Kong*);
6. grief (*Bei*);
7. fright (*Jing*).

These seven emotional factors become pathogenic only when they are intense and persistent or if the individual is hyper-sensitive to the stimulations (see **five emotions** and **seven injuries**).

---

seven injuries [*Qi shang* 七伤 *Thất thu'o'ng*], excessive emotions may injure the spiritual resources:
1. *extreme fear* injures *Jing* (essence of life);
2. *anxiety* damages *Shen* (spirit);
3. *excessive joy* is harmful to *Po* (animal spirit);
4. *sadness* injures *Hun* (soul);
5. *melancholy* damages *Yi* (mind);
6. *violent anger* injures *Zhi* (desire);
7. *excessive tiredness* damages *Qi* (vital energy).

seven odd pulses [*Qi guai mai* 七怪脉 *Thất quái mạch*], are unusual kinds of pulse indicating impending death:
1. **pecking,** 2. **fish swimming,** 3. **shrimp darting,** 4. **boiling,** 5. **dripping,** 6. **flicking,** 7. **snapping,** (see appropriate heading for details).

seven openings [*Qi qiao* 七窍 *Thất khiêú*], are the major or upper openings on the head and face: ears, eyes, nostrils, mouth which are among the usual points of observation on the patient for diagnostic purpose.

seven passes [*Qi chong men* 七冲门 *Thất xung môn*], along the alimentary tract are:
1. lips or flying gate (*Fei men*); 2. teeth or front gate (*Hu men*); 3. epiglottis or suction gate (*Xi men*); 4. cardia or entrance to the stomach (*Ben men*); 5. pylorus or exit from the stomach (*You men*); 6. ileocaecal junction or door (*lan men*); 7. anus or animal spirit gate (*Po men*).

seven-star needle [*Qi xing zhen* 七星针 *Thất tinh châm*], is a special kind made with seven short needles attached vertically to the end of a 12-15 cm long stick to tap lightly at the skin surface of the affected area or along certain lines (Figure 42a) (see **plum blossom acupuncture** and **tapping**).

shedding of fur [*Bo tai* 剥苔 *Bác dài*], a normal tongue should be clean, moist with normal papillae. Atrophy of the papillae is a sign of ill health.
1. *Partial atrophy* or geographical tongue may be the manifestation of parasitosis.

2. *Total atrophy* of the papillae suggests deficiency of the **liver** and **kidney** *Qi*.

Shen Nong (about 2700 BC) [神农 *Thần Nông*], second of the five legendary emperors in the Chinese history. As he invented the cart and plough and taught his people to till, he was called Shen Nong or Divine Farmer and was considered the Father of agriculture. He was also believed to be the author of the Shen Nong's *Herbal* (*Shen Nong ben cao jing*), the earliest *materia medica* in which 365 kinds of drugs were listed and divided into three classes: superior, inferior and medium.

---

shiatsu, Japanese term for finger (*Shi*) pressure (*Atsu*). It is a form of massage done almost entirely with the balls of the thumbs and is used in a wide variety of diseases. This ancient Japanese therapy is said to have appeared at the same time as acupuncture in China and is very popular in Japan.

---

shock, see **collapse.**

---

short pulse [*Duan mai* 短脉 *Đoản mạch*], is usually felt in only one position, indicating deficient *Qi*.

---

shrimp darting pulse [*Xia you mai* 虾游脉 *Hà du mạch*], is weak, darting before disappearing. It is one of the seven pulses indicating impending death.

Shu **(transporting) points** [*Shu xue* 俞穴 *Du huyệt*], may refer to:
1. the points where *Qi* and blood are pouring in. The most important of these points are located on the back, at either side of the vertebral column and are called **back *shu* points.** They are points where *Qi* of the respective *Zang Fu* organs is infused,
2. the *Shu*-stream point, one of the five *Shu* points, where *Qi* is pouring along.

---

six channels [*Liu jing* 六经 *Lục kinh*], refer to the following channels: greater *Yang* (*Taiyang*), lesser *Yang* (*Shaoyang*), sunlight *Yang* (*Yangming*), greater *Yin* (*Taiyin*), absolute *Yin* (*Jueyin*), lesser *Yin* (*Shaoyin*).

---

six channels, diagnosis based on [*Liu jing bian zheng* 六经辨证 *Lục kinh biện chú'ng*], a theory developed by Zhang Ji (AD 150?-219?), author of the *Treatise on Febrile and Miscellaneous Diseases* (*Shang han za bing lun*), concerning the course of the diseases caused by the **external pathogenic factors.** According to the author, all diseases caused by the external pathogenic factors are characterized by fever and proceed progressively but not necessarily in a definite sequence, through six evolutive stages or six channels:

1. *greater Yang* (*Taiyang*), this first stage marks the onset of the disease and is characterized by fear of cold or wind, fever, headache and floating pulse. After this stage, the pathogenic factor moves either to the lesser *Yang* (*Shaoyang*) or to the sunlight *Yang* (*Yangming*).

2. *Sunlight Yang* (*Yangming*), this stage corresponds to the internal development of the disease and is characterized by fever, thirst, perspiration, irritability, rapid pulse,

3. *Lesser Yang* (*Shaoyang*), symptoms of this stage include chills and fever, nausea, bitter taste in the mouth, lack of appetite, irrtability,

4. *Greater Ying* (*Taiyin*), abdominal distension, lack of thirst, poor appetite, vomiting, diarrhoea are among signs of this stage,

5. *Lesser Yin* (*Shaoyin*), this stage is more serious and is characterized by drowsiness, feeble pulse, aversion to cold, cold extremities, lack of fever,

6. *Absolute Yin* (*Jueyin*), it is the most serious stage.

This theory of diagnosis based on the six evolutive stages or channels constitutes the basis for treatment of febrile diseases of external origin.

---

six excessive atmospheric influences [*Liu yin* 六淫 *Lục dâm*], are **cold, wind, summer heat, dampness, dryness** and **heat** (fire, mild heat), known as six exogenous factors, may be harmful to the health if excessive. (see appropriate heading for details).

---

six pairs of exterior interior related channels [*Liu he* 六合 *Lục hộp*], are: lung — large intestine, kidney — urinary bladder, liver —

gall bladder, heart — small intestine, pericardium — three heater, spleen — stomach.

---

six *Yang* pulses [*Liu Yang mai* 六阳脉 *Lục Dươ'ng mạch*], refer to six full and big pulses felt on three positions of both hands, due to physiological abnormalities, not to pathological conditions.

---

six *Yin* pulses [*Liu Yin mai* 六阴脉 *Lục Âm mạch*], refer to six weak and thready pulses felt on three positions of both hands, due to physiological abnormalities, not to pathological conditions.

---

skin [*Pi fu* 皮肤 *Bì phu*], literally, the term '*Pi*' means cover, wrapper, envelope which could be skin, leather, hide, peel etc. '*Fu*' refers to the skin including the layer of fatty tissue just beneath. The term '*Pi fu*' refers to the cover of the body surface which includes the epidermis, dermis and subcutaneous fatty tissue. The lustre of the skin depends on the condition of the lungs. 'The lungs dominate the skin and hair'.

---

slippery pulse [*Hua mai* 滑脉 *Hoạt mạch*], fluid and smooth, is seen in cases of excess of **dampness, phlegm,** stagnation of food and also in pregnant women.

---

slow pulse [*Chi mai* 迟脉 *Trì mạch*], has less than four beats per physician's respiration, usually seen in cases of **cold** or obstruction of the *Yang* function. This type of pulse may also be seen in some athletes.

---

small intestine [*Xiao chang* 小肠 *Tiểu tru'o'ṅg*], is one of the six *Fu* organs. The main function of the small intestine is to complete the process of digestion. It absorbs the nutritive substances and a small amount of water. The residues and a large amount of fluid pass into the large intestine to be transformed into faeces. It had been once believed that the urine came from the small intestine.

---

snapping pulse [*Jie suo mai* 解素脉 *Giải tác mạch*], arrhythmic pulse resembling the snapping of a cord, is one of the seven pulses indicating impending death.

soggy pulse [*Ru mai* 濡脉 *Nhu Mạch*], soft, superficial and thready, like a thread floating on the surface of the water and can be felt on light pressure. It is the manifestation of **dampness** or deficiency in *Qi* and blood.

solidity of the stomach [*Wei shi* 胃实 *Vị thiệt*], a condition due to accumulation of **heat** in the **stomach** resulting in loss of fluid and disturbance of the functions of the stomach which becomes inactive, hard. Symptoms are stomach pain, eructation, constipation etc.

son, see **child**.

soul [*Hun* 魂 *Hồn*], one of the five spiritual resources dwelling in the liver which maintains mental balance. According to Chinese belief, the human body is dominated by two souls, one of a high spiritual nature called *Hun* and the other of a low animal nature called *Po* or animal spirit. It is believed that at the moment of death, the soul or *Hun* escapes through a hole at the top of the head called fontanelle or *Xin men*. This also happens when people dream. The expression 'losing one's *Hun*' refers to an unstable mental condition or a state of excessive fright. The point UB47 or soul gate (*Hun Men*), located three *Cun* lateral to the lower border of the spinous process of the ninth thoracic vertebra, is indicated in pain in the hypochondriac region, chest, back, vomiting, diarrhoea, liver diseases.

source (*Yuan*) points [*Yuan xue* 源 *Nguyên huyệt*], each of the twelve main channels has a source (*Yuan*) point located near the wrist and the ankle (Figure 51; table 5). On the *Yin* channel, this point coincides with the *Shu*-Stream point. These source points are of great importance in diagnosis and treatment of diseases of the **channels** and **internal organs**. They are indicated in both deficiency and excess syndromes of their respective related organs and can be used either separately or in conjunction with the **connecting (*Luo*) points**.

123

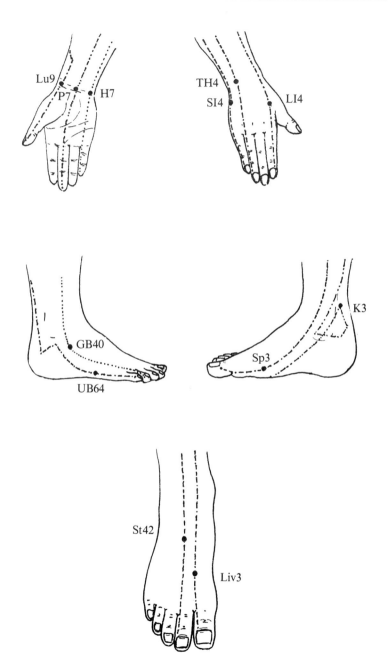

Figure 51: Source (*Yuan*) points

source *Qi* [*Yuan Qi* 元 气 *Nguyên khí*],   also called congenital Qi, is the *Qi* of the **kidney**, inherited from the parents and related to the function of reproduction.

---

spirit [*Shen* 神 *Thần*],   has special reference to the outward appearance reflecting the mental state or facial expression: complexion, posture, alertness and shine of the eyes, speech, hearing, clarity of thought, consciousness etc. According to the Chinese concept, the spirit has also a material aspect since the child's spirit is inherited from his parents. It is the fundamental substance of the human body, nourished by *Qi* and blood and dwelling in the heart. 'The heart houses and controls the spirit, affects the face.' *Qi*, *Jing* and *Shen*, important factors of life and death, are considered the 'three precious things' (*San bao*). Disharmony of the spirit is manifested by signs such as dull eyes, lack of alertness, impaired hearing, abnormal speech, impaired memory, delusion, madness in severe cases. The acupuncture points H7, *Shen men* (spirit gate) and UB44, *Shen tang* (spirit hall) are particularly indicated in heart diseases.

---

spleen [*Pi* 脾 *Tỳ*],   one of the five *Zang* organs, the main physiological functions of the spleen are:
1. digestion and absorption of food;
2. controlling the circulation of blood;
3. dominating the muscles;
4. opening into the mouth;
5. ruling over the liver;
6. generating the lungs since the spleen nourishes the flesh which strengthens the lungs;
7. controlling the idea.

---

stagnant noxious dampness [*Shi du* 湿毒 *Thấp độc*],   may cause various symptoms depending on the affected organs. Rectal bleeding occurs if the stagnation is in the intestine. Carbuncles or boils on the legs are manifestations of stagnant **dampness** in the muscles and skin of the lower limbs.

---

stagnant *Qi* [*Qi zhi* 气滞 *Khí trệ*],   in organs or channels causes impairment of the affected organs or the areas related to the affected channels. The causes of the stagnation may be emotional disturbances, trauma or **external pathogenic factors.** The chief manifestations are pain and distension. Dyspnoea, cough, chest distension occur in cases of stagnant *Qi* in the lungs. Abdominal distension, lower abdominal pain, painful and swollen breast and external genitalia are manifestations of the stagnation of *Qi* in the **liver.**

---

stagnation, six kinds [*Liu yu* 六郁 *Lục uất*], which may be harmful to the health are, namely, stagnation of **Qi, blood, dampness, fire, phlegm** and food. The first two are the most important.

---

stomach [*Wei* 胃 *Vị*], one of the six *Fu* organs, sometimes called granary since the stomach is a transitional storing place of the ingested food. It is one of the four seas in the human body: 'Sea of Water and Grain'. According to traditional Chinese medicine, the **stomach** and the **spleen** are both main organs of digestion and absorption. It associates closely with the **lungs** and **kidneys** since the downward flow moves to the kidneys to be transformed into urine. In Chinese, the term '*Wei Wan*' means either the epigastrium or the cavity of the **stomach.** The acupuncture points Cv10 (*Xia Wan*), Cv12 (*Zhong Wan*) and Cv13 (*Shang Wan*) or lower, middle and upper gastric cavity respectively, are particularly indicated in gastric pain, abdominal distension, vomiting.

---

stone needles, see **needles.**

---

stuck needle [*Zhi zhen* 滯針 *Trệ châm*], is one which is difficult or impossible to rotate, lift or thrust. This accident in acupuncture may be due to:

1. muscular spasm: wait a few minutes before rotating and removing the needle;

2. entanglement of the fibrous tissue: rotate the needle gently and slowly.

---

summer heat [*Shu* 暑 *Thử*], is one of the **six exogenous factors** or atmospheric influences. Diseases caused by the pathogenic summer heat occur only in the summer and are often due to prolonged exposure to the hot sun or staying in a hot and poorly ventilated room. It is a *Yang* pathogenic factor which consumes *Qi* and *Yin* and may disturb the mind. Symptoms are excessive sweating, thirst, shortness of breath, fatigue, delirium or coma in severe cases. Conditions due to **summer heat** and **dampness** (humid heat) are manifested by dizziness, nausea, diarrhoea.

Sun Si-miao (AD 581-682) [孙思邈 *Tôn Tử Mạo*],   a prominent physician of the Tang dynasty, and author of *The Prescriptions Worth a Thousand Gold (Qian jin yao fang)* in thirty volumes and *The supplement to the Prescriptions Worth a Thousand Gold (Qian jin yi fang)* also in thirty volumes. His maxim in acupuncture is 'Puncture wherever there is tenderness', thus the origin of the *Ah Shi* (ah yes) points.

---

sunlight *Yang* syndrome [*Yangming bing* 阳明病 *Du'o'ng minh bệnh*],   has two types:
.1. syndrome of sunlight *Yang* channel characterized by fever, thirst, perspiration, intolerance to heat;
2. syndrome of sunlight *Yang Fu* organs with manifestations such as fever, delirium, abdominal pain, constipation etc. (see **six channels, diagnosis based on**).

---

superficial defensive system syndrome [*Wei Feng zheng* 卫分证 *Vệ phu'o'ng chửng*],   shows conditions due to the involvement of the superficial part of the body in early stage of an epidemic febrile disease. The main manifestations are fever, headache, general aching, hypohydrosis, rapid pulse etc.

Supplement to The Prescriptions Worth a Thousand Gold [*Qian jin yi fang* 千金翼方 *Thiên kim dực phu'o'ng*],   written by Sun Si-miao in AD 682 in thirty volumes, the subjects include various medical branches such as herbalism, **pulse feeling, acupuncture, moxibustion.**

---

supreme ultimate,   see *Tai Ji.*

---

sweat [*Han* 汗 *Hãn*],   is the end product of the transformation of the lung air (*Fei Qi*) and is exuded as useless waste matter through the sweat pores.

---

swollen lips [*Chun zhong* 唇肿 *Thần thũng*] a condition due to accumulation of **heat** in the **spleen** and **stomach** or food poisoning.

---

syncope [*Jue* 厥 *Quyết*], is a sudden loss of consciousness mostly due to poor health with emotional disturbance and exhaustion. In this condition, *Qi* and blood of the twelve channels can't move to the head, the *Yang Qi* is unable to reach the extremities, the nourishing and defensive *Qi* are out of their normal courses.

Syncope is of two types: *deficiency* (*Xu*), symptoms are shallow breathing, excessive sweating, pallor, cold extremities, thready pulse, mouth agape; *excess* (*Shi*), coarse breathing, rigid extremities, forceful pulse, clenched jaws are the main manifestations.

Systematic Compilation of the Internal Medicine [*Lei jing* 类经 *Loại kinh*], a reclassification and commentary of *Nei* Jing, compiled by Zhang Jing-yue and published in AD1624. This important reference book consists of twelve categories (*Lei*) including hygiene, pulse, channels, *Yin Yang* theory, acupuncture, treatment of diseases etc.

Szuma Chien (BC145-c.90) [司马迁 *Tu' Mã Thiên*] a great historian, author of *The Historical Records* (*Shih Chi*). At the end of his career, he fell into disgrace and suffered the castration punishment.

T

***Tai Ji,* supreme ultimate** [太极 *Thái cực*], is the Chinese Taoist symbol representing the balance of *Yin* and *Yang* (Figure 25). It is believed that *Yin* and *Yang* come from the **supreme ultimate** which, according to Chinese philosophy, is the source of all reality. The circle represents the whole and is divided into *Yin* (black) and *Yang* (white). The small dots of reverse shading refer to the *Yang* in *Yin* and the *Yin* in *Yang*. The curve separating the black and white areas indicates the continuous movement of *Yin* and *Yang*: they create, control and transform into each other.

---

tapping [*Qiao* 敲 *Xao*], is a method of treatment using the plum blossom or seven-star needle to tap the skin surface. Tapping may be light or heavy according to the constitution of the patient and the type of disease. The duration of the tapping and the number of the taps vary according to the individual patient. The location depends on the pathological condition, the distribution of the channels and the location of the prescribed points. This method of treatment, particularly suitable for women, children or those who are sensitive to pain, is prescribed in headache, insomnia, disorders of the stomach and intestine, chronic diseases in women, certain kinds of skin diseases.

---

tardy pulse [*Huan mai* 緩脉 *Hoãn mạch*], has four beats to one cycle of the physician's respiration and even rhythm, seen in the normal condition. However this kind of pulse may be found in cases with **dampness** and dysfunction of the **stomach** and **spleen**.

---

teeth [*Ya* 牙 *Nha*], also called front gate (*Hu men*), are one of the seven passes of the alimentary tract. The teeth are considered 'the surplus of bones' and are ruled by the **kidneys**. When there is recurrent trouble with the teeth, the function of the kidneys should be investigated. The state of the teeth reflects the conditions of the internal organs: *dry teeth* and gums indicate **heat** in the stomach; deficient kidney *Yin* is manifested by the teeth which look like *dry bones*; *grinding* the teeth at night is a sign of **heat**.

---

ten important points of inspection, see **inspection**.

---

ten questions, see **interrogation.**

---

tendon [*Jin* 筋 *Cân*], like many other anatomical terms in traditional Chinese medicine, doesn't have exactly the same meaning as that of Western anatomists. The term '*Jin*' may refer to:
1. muscle;
2. tendon, sinew;
3. veins which are visible under the skin;
4. anything resembling a tendon or vein.

The condition of the tendons in the body depends on the liver: 'The liver rules the tendons'. In cases of deficiency in liver blood, spasms, stiffness and numbness of the limbs may occur.

---

thready pulse [*Xi mai* 细脉 *Ty mạch*], is feeble and thin like a silk thread, perceptible only on hard pressure, indicating deficiency in *Qi*, blood and body fluid.

---

three-barrier pulse [*San guan zhi mai* 三关之脉 *Tam quan chi mạch*], the proximal, middle and distal segments of the under three-year-old child's index finger are called Wind barrier (*Feng Guan*), *Qi* barrier (*Qi Guan*) and life barrier (*Ming Guan*) respectively (Figure 52). In children under three years old, the diagnosis can be made by examining the minor veins of the three segments or 'barriers' of the index fingers.

---

three-edge needle [*San leng zhen* 三棱针 *Tam lăng châm*], is a special needle with triangular head and sharp tip used for bleeding purposes (Figure 42d).

---

three heater [*San jiao* 三焦 *Tam tiêu*], '*San*' means three and '*Jiao*' can be translated as heater, burner, warmer, burning space etc. Although many explanations have been put forward, none gives an accurate definition of this Chinese term. According to Nei Jing, the **three heater** is a kind of sewage system without any particular form. In *Difficult Classic* (*Nan Jing*), it is called 'the sixth *Yang* organ in charge of supporting different kinds of *Qi* in the body'. Some others maintain that the function of the **three heater** is transforming and transporting the nutritive substances

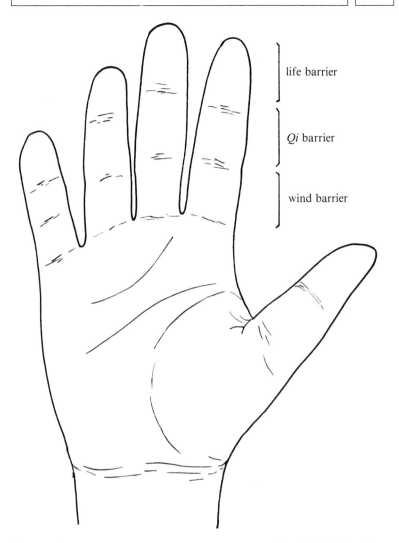

life barrier

Qi barrier

wind barrier

Figure 52: Three barriers of the under three-year-old child's index finger used in diagnosis

as well as eliminating the waste materials. The **three heater** is probably best regarded as the generalization of the function of some internal organs which regulate the water in the human body. As its name suggests, the **three heater** has three parts:

the upper heater, relating to the chest, is the generalization of the function of the **heart** and **lungs** in transporting *Qi* and blood to different parts of the body; *the middle heater*, corresponding to the epigastrium, is the generalization of the function of the **spleen** and **stomach** in digestion and absorption; *the lower heater* represents the hypogastric region and is the generalization of the function of the **kidneys** and **urinary bladder** in regulation of water metabolism. Although the **three heater** is not a substantial organ, it still plays an important role in acupuncture. It has also is own channel connecting with the **pericardium channel** with which it is externally/internally related.

The main pathological manifestations of the three heater channel include: abdominal distension, oedema, dysuria, deafness, tinnitus, swelling of the cheeks, sore throat, shoulder pain, pain in the lateral aspect of the arm.

---

three-portion and nine-area pulse taking method [*San bu jiu hou* 三部九候 *Tam bộ cửu hậu*], has two explanations:

1. It was a method of general check-up in ancient times. The physician takes the pulse of the upper, middle and lower areas of the three portions of the body namely the head, the upper and lower limbs.

2. Over the radial artery on the wrist, for pulse feeling, there are three positions called inch, bar and cubit. At each position, the pulse can be felt at three levels of pressure: superficial, middle and deep. Feeling the pulse at all positions and levels is equivalent to the general check-up.

---

three precious things [*San bao* 三宝 *Tam bảo*], are *Jing* (essence of life), *Qi* (vital energy) and *Shen* (spirit) which are intimately interrelated and are predominant factors of life and death.

---

three therapeutic methods [*San fa* 三法 *Tam pháp*], are: diaphoresis, emesis and purgation.

---

throat [*Hou* 喉 *Hầu*], reflects not only the conditions of the **lungs** but also the conditions of the other organs:

red, swollen and painful throat or tonsils: **heat** specially in the **lungs** or **stomach;** *ulceration* of the throat: extreme **heat;** *sensation of a lump* in the throat: stagnation of **liver** *Qi.*

---

tie (*Wei*) channels, see *Yin* and *Yang Tie* (*Wei*) **channels.**

---

tight pulse [*Jin mai* 紧脉 *Kiên mạch*], is strong like a cord and vibrating. More elastic than the wiry pulse, this kind of pulse is seen in cases with excess, stagnation, **cold** in the exterior and interior.

---

tongue examination [*She zhen* 舌诊 *Thiệt chẩn*], plays an important

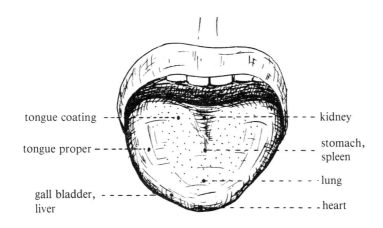

tongue coating -- -- -- kidney

tongue proper -- -- -- stomach, spleen

gall bladder, -- -- -- lung
liver -- -- -- heart

Figure 53: The tongue and the corresponding organs

part in the diagnosis. Since there is close relation between the tongue and the **internal organs, channels, collaterals, Qi, blood** and body fluid, any disorders of these may be manifested on the tongue. In early Chinese medical texts, various types of tongue and their significance have been mentioned. Nei Jing described many types of tongue and in the *Mirror of the tongue for Cold induced diseases* (*Shang han she jian*) published in AD1668, Zhang Deng described 120 types of tongue. The tongue is divided into the tongue proper and the tongue coating. A normal tongue should be of proper size, light red in colour, free in motion. The coating is thin, whitish, moist. The conditions of some internal organs are reflected in different parts of the tongue: the tip, middle, root and borders of the tongue correspond to the **heart, spleen** and **stomach, kidneys, liver** and **gall bladder** respectively (Figure 53). The examination of the tongue must include its movement and size, its surface (proper and coating):

A. Tongue proper:

1. *pale: deficiency of Yang Qi,* **blood,** invasion of **external cold;**

2. *abnormal bright red*: due either to invasion of pathogenic **heat** (excess type) or depletion of *Yin* fluid (deficiency type);

3. *deep red*: severe febrile diseases or chronic diseases;

4. *purplish*: stagnation of *Qi* and **blood;**

5. *thorny*: hyperactivity of pathogenic **heat;**

6. *cracked*: loss of kidney essence (*Jing*), hyperactivity of **fire** due to *Yin* deficiency, depletion of body fluid by excessive **heat.**

B. Tongue coating:

1. *white: thin*, normal or invasion of the **lungs** by **wind cold;** *thick*, food retention; *sticky*, invasion by **cold damp** or retention of **phlegm damp;** *dry*, invasion by pestilential factor.

2. *Yellow: thin*, invasion of the **lungs** by **wind heat;** *thick*, food retention; *sticky*, accumulated **damp heat** or blockage of the **lungs** by **phlegm heat;** *dry*, accumulation of **heat** in the **stomach** and intestine.

3. *Greyish black*: *moist*, retention of **cold damp;** *dry*, depletion of body fluid by excessive **heat** or hyperactive **fire.**

4. *peeling*, partial (geographical tongue) or total, chronic diseases.

C. Size and motility:

1. *shortened or contracted*, **cold** or **heat;**

2. *sluggish*, usually curled and stiff in apoplexy, encephalitis;

3. *swollen*, deficiency of functional activities of the **spleen;**

4. *wry*, onset of internal **wind** of the **liver;**

5. *flabby*, deficiency of *Qi* and *Yang* with retention of **phlegm damp;**

6. *rigid*: invasion of exogenous *heat*, damage of liver *Yin* by excessive **heat** or obstruction of collaterals by **wind phlegm.**

---

tonification point [*Bu xue* 补 穴 *Bổ huyệt*], of a channel is the 'mother' point of its own phase e.g. the **lung** belongs to metal, the preceding phase or 'mother' is earth, the tonification point is therefore Lu9 (Table 9).

---

tonifying mother, see **mother-child relationship.**

---

touching [*Qie zhen* 切诊 *Thiết chẩn*], is the most important of the four methods of diagnosis in traditional Chinese medicine and consists of:

1. *Feeling the pulse* constitutes the basis of the traditional Chinese medicine. The characters of the pulse reflect the condition of each organ as well as the balance between different organs.

2. *Palpation* of the channels, points and different parts of the body: a) Certain diseases may be manifested by tenderness or other abnormal reactions along the course of the involved channels or at certain points. (e.g. Tenderness at Lu1 or nodule at UB13 may be found in lung diseases.) b) Palpation of certain parts of the body may be helpful. (e.g. Pain in the right lower abdomen suggests appendicitis, resulting from stagnation of *Qi* and blood.

---

transporting (*Shu*) points, see *Shu* **points.**

Treatise on Fevers and Miscellaneous Diseases [*Shang han za bing lun* 伤寒杂病论 *Thu'o'ng hàn tạp bệnh luận*], written by Zhang Ji (AD150?-219?) in sixteen volumes, it explains the diagnosis and treatment of cold induced diseases and other miscellaneous disorders. The book was later reorganized by Wang Shu-he in the Jin dynasty and, in the Song dynasty, it was divided into two books: *Treatise on Febrile Diseases* or *Cold Induced Diseases* (*Shang han lun*), and *Synopsis of Prescriptions of the Golden Chamber* (*Jin kui yao lue fang lun*).

Treatise on Febrile Diseases [*Shang han lun* 伤寒论 *Thu'o'ng hàn luận*], the revised edition of Zhang Ji's book (see above) by Wan Shu-he (in 10 volumes) in which febrile diseases are analysed and differentiated in accordance with the theory of six pairs of channels.

---

twelve joints [*Shi er jie* 十二节 *Thập nhị tiết*], refer to the joints of the shoulder girdle, elbow and wrist of the upper limbs and those of the thigh, knee and ankle of the lower limbs.

---

two *Yin* [*Er Yin* 二 阴 *Nhị Âm*], refers to the external genitalia including the urethral orifice and the **anus.**

---

typhoid fever [*Shang han* 伤 寒 *Thu'o'ng hàn*], is so called since it had been believed that the disease was caused by evil **cold.** The Chinese term literally means injured by **cold.**

U

---

upper heater, see **three heater.**

---

upper openings, see **seven openings.**

---

upper part of the stomach [*Shang wan* 上 脘 *Thu'ọ'ng quản*], the Chinese term refers to: 1. the upper part of the stomach, the cardia area; and 2. the acupuncture point Cv13, indicated in gastric pain, regurgitation, vomiting.

---

urinary bladder [*Pang guang* 膀 胱 *Bàng quang*], one of the six *Fu* organs. It had been believed that the urine, from the small intestine, enters the urinary bladder through a hole at the top of it. The main physiological function of the urinary bladder is to store the urine temporarily until its discharge. This function can be carried out thanks to the **kidney** *Qi.*

---

uterus [*Zi gong* 子 宫 *Tủ' cung*], is one of the six extraordinary or curious organs. Its main function is to nourish the fetus and to control menstruation. Some internal organs and channels are related to the uterus: **kidneys:** the regular menstruation and the growth of the fetus depend on the essence (*Jing*) of the kidneys; **liver:** responsible for the normal menstruation; **conception vessel** and **penetrating channel:** both originate in the uterus. The conception vessel nourishes the fetus. The penetrating channel, by regulating *Qi* and blood of the twelve main channels, influences the menstruation. The extraordinary point Zigong is particularly indicated in prolapse of the uterus, irregular menstruation.

The Chinese term literally means child (*Zi*) palace (*gong*). The other name is blood chamber (*Xue shi*).

V

vertigo [*Xuan yun* 眩晕 *Huyên vụng*],　may be caused by: 1. dysfunction of the kidney affecting the **liver**; 2. interior retention of **phlegm damp**; 3. insufficiency of the Sea of marrow in the head due to the deficiency of *Qi* and **blood**. Symptoms and signs depend on the etiology: tinnitus, nausea, rapid pulse: dysfunction of the **kidneys**; vomiting, sensation of fullness in the chest and epigastric region: interior retention of **phlegm damp**; lassitude, palpitation, weak pulse: deficient *Qi* and **blood.**

vibrating the needle [*Zhen chan zhen* 震颤针 *Chân chiên châm*], is a method of inducing the needle reaction (*De Qi*) by a quick lift and thrust movement with small amplitude.

vital area [*Gao huang* 膏肓 *Cao hoang*],　'Gao' refers to the area below the heart and 'Huang' is the region located between the heart and the diaphragm. Lesion of this area will be fatal. The Chinese expression 'The disease has reached *Gao Huang*' means the situation is hopeless, the disease is at its final stage. The acupuncture point UB43 (*Gaohuangshu* or Vitals Shu) is particularly prescribed in chronic diseases with general debility.

W

Wang Ji (AD 1463-1539) [汪机 *Uông Co'*], author of several medical books such as *Catechism of Acupuncture and Moxibustion (Zhen Jiu wen de)*, *Surgery with illustrations (Wai ke li li)*, *Principles of Medicine (Yi xue li li)*.

Wang Wei-yi (about AD 987-1067) [王维 – *Vu'o'ng Duy Nhât*], author of *The Illustrated Manual on the Points for Acupuncture and Moxibustion as Found on the Bronze Figure (Tong ren yu xue zhen jiu tu jing)* published in AD 1027. He studied in detail the acupuncture points and marked out a total of 657 points. He sponsored the casting of two life size hollow bronze figures on the surface of which were marked the channels and acupuncture points (Figure 54). The figure was filled with water which can flow out through the acupuncture points and was used for teaching and testing candidates.

Wang Xi (about AD 210-285) [王熙 *Vu'o'ng Hy*], other name Wang Shu-he (*Vu'o'ng Thúc Hoà*), was the author of the *Pulse Classic*, the first comprehensive book on sphygmology now extant in China. He perfected and systemized the art of **pulse feeling** and stressed the use of all the four methods of diagnosis namely inspection, listening and smelling, interrogation, touching.

warm heat [*Wen re* 温热 *Ôn nhiệt*], refers to: 1. the pathogenic factor attacking insidiously and prevailing in winter, spring and autumn; 2. the epidemic febrile diseases; 3. the epidemic febrile diseases caused exclusively by **heat**.

water [*Shui* 水 *Thủy*], one of the **five phases** symbolizing the **kidneys**, **bones** and **ears**. According to the theory of five phases, water (kidney) promotes wood (liver), acts on fire (heart) and counteracts earth (spleen) (see **five phases**).

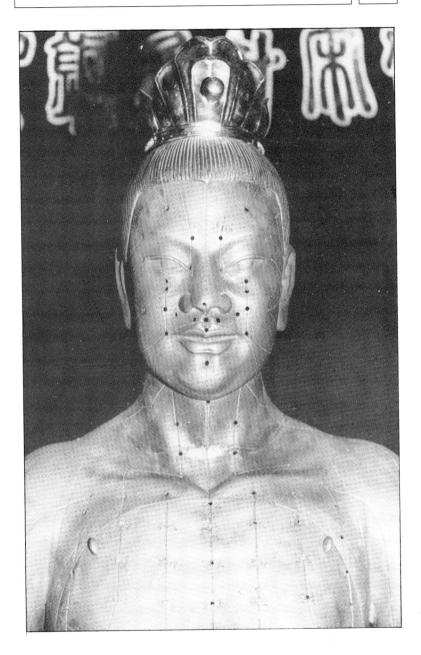

Figure 54: The bronze model showing acupuncture points made in AD 1027 (by courtesy of the WHO)

weak pulse [*Ruo mai* 弱 脉 *Nhược mạch*], is deep and soft, seen in case of general debility.

Wei **channel,** see *Yin* and *Yang* **tie channels.**

---

white complexion [*Bai se* 白 色 *Bạch sắć*], is caused by debility, indicating **cold** and deficiency in blood.

---

wind [*Feng* 风 *Phong*], is difficult to define satisfactorily. In Chinese medicine, the term wind doesn't refer to the movement of air. Although immaterial, wind does have the quality of movement, it changes and moves continuously. Wind is considered one of the six **exogenous pathogenic factors,** prevailing in spring, occuring in gusts, attacking the organs directly or indirectly. It is usually associated with other pathogenic factors, e.g. wind cold, damp wind etc. Wind is of two types: *external wind* (*Wai Feng*), diseases caused by external wind are characterized by a sudden onset, e.g. common cold; *internal wind* (*Nei Feng*), diseases caused by internal wind are chronic and characterized by symptoms such as shakiness, fainting, stiffness, cramps, convulsions (e.g. Parkinson's disease).

---

windstroke, see **apoplexy.**

---

wiry pulse [*Xian mai* 弦 脉 *Huyền mạch*], is forceful and taut feeling like pressing on a tremulous musical instrument string. This type of pulse is usually seen in liver diseases or severe pain.

---

withdrawing, needle [*Chu zhen* 出针 *Xuất châm*], to prevent bleeding at the site of puncture and aftersensation, rotate the needle back and forth gently before withdrawing it then press the puncture site with cotton ball.

---

wood [*Mu* 木 *Mộc*], one of the **five phases** symbolizing the **liver,** sinew and **eyes.** According to the theory of five phases, wood (liver) promotes fire (heart), acts on earth (spleen) and counteracts metal (lung) (see **five phases**).

---

wooden tongue [*Mu she* 木舌 *Mộc thiệt*], is swollen and hardened due to excessive **fire** in the **heart** or accumulated **heat** in the heart and **spleen.**

Wu You-Xing (AD 1582-1652) [吴有性 *Ngô Hu'ũ' Tính*], author of *The Treatise on Epidemic Febrile Diseases* (*Wen yi lun*) in two volumes, dealing with several kinds of epidemic diseases prevalent at that time in many parts of China. His theory of Perverse *Qi* (*Li Qi*) is important in the aetiology of communicable diseases.

X

Xi (cleft) points, see **accumulating points.**

Xu Shu-wei (AD 1079-1154) [许叔微 *Hú'a Thúc Vĩ*], a famous physician in the twelfth century, and author of several medical books. He prepared graphic illustrations of thirty-six types of pulse based on Zhang Zhong-jing's work, put forward the theory on the use of medicines in relation to the intensity of the disease.

---

xyphoid process [*Jiu wei* 鸠尾 *Cu'u Vĩ*], so-called since the xyphoid process resembles the dove (*Jiu*) tail (*Wei*). Also refers to the acupuncture point Cv15 below the xyphoid process.

Y

Yang **heel channel** [*Yang qiao jing* 阳跟经 *Du'o'ng căn kinh*], so called since this extra channel starts from the lateral side of the heel (*Qiao*) and ends at point GB20 (Figure 55). Epilepsy and insomnia are among the pathological manifestations of the channel.

Yang Ji-zhou (**AD 1522-1620**) [杨继洲 *Du'o'ng Kế Châu*], author of *The Compendium of Acupuncture and Moxibustion* (*Zhen jiu da cheng*) published in AD 1602, a comprehensive and practical book which mentioned the use of moxibustion on the ear apex to treat cataract.

Yang **tie channel** [*Yang wei jing* 阳维经 *Du'o'ng duy kinh*], one of the eight extra channels, starts from the heel, connects with all the Yang channels and ends at Gv15 (Figure 55). The Chinese term '*Wei*' means tie, connection. The *Wei* channels connect with and regulate all the *Yang* or *Yin* channels. The main pathological manifestations of this channel are fever and chills.

Yin **diseases** [*Yin bing* 阴病 *Âm bệnh*], refer to: the diseases of deficiency symptom complex or cold nature due to low body resistance or deficient vital function; and the diseases relating to the three *Yin* channels.

Yin **heel channel** [*Yin qiao jing* 阴跟经 *Âm căn kinh*], one of the eight extra channels, starting from the posterior aspect of the navicular bone, communicates with the *Yang* heel channel after reaching the inner canthus (Figure 56). Hypersomnia is its main pathological manifestation.

Yin **tie channel** [*Yin wei jing* 阴维经 *Âm duy kinh*], so called since this extra channel connects with and regulates all the *Yin* channels. It starts from the medial aspect of the leg and ends at the neck (Figure 56). Cardialgia is its main pathological manifestation.

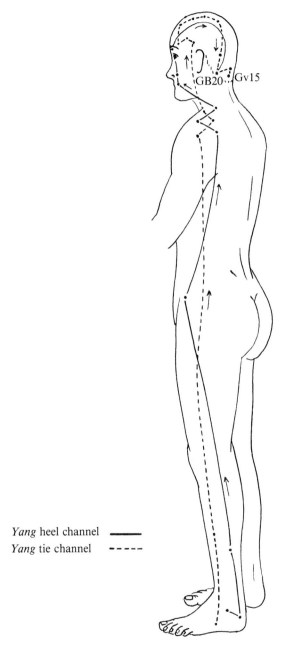

Figure 55: The *Yang* heel (*Qiao*) and the *Yang* tie (*Wei*) channels

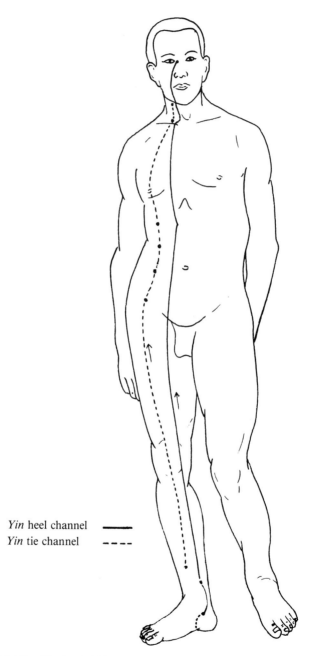

Yin heel channel ——
Yin tie channel ----

Figure 56: The *Yin* heel (*Qiao*) and the *Yin* tie (*Wei*) channels

Yin Yang concept [*Yin Yang shuo* 阴阳说 *Âm Du'o'ng thuyêt*], is an ancient philosophical concept used in traditional Chinese medicine. According to this concept, in the universe there are two fundamental principles or forces called *Yin* and *Yang*, ever opposing and supplementing each other. *Yang* is seen as hot, male, heaven, light, active, exterior while *Yin* is associated with cold, female, earth, dark, passive, interior. All aspects and phenomena of life such as change, birth, growth, death etc. can exist only thanks to the interactions of these two forces. Harmony can be found in the natural world and in human body when there is a balance between these two principles. In case of imbalance or disharmony of *Yin* and *Yang*, diseases occur. This theory of *Yin* and *Yang*, is well illustrated by the traditional Chinese Taoist symbol (Figure 25) (see *Tai Ji* or **supreme ultimate**).

Yin Yang **guiding symptom complexes, diagnosis based on** [*Yin Yang bian zheng* 阴阳辨证 *Âm Duong biên chúng*], is used to explain some of the pathological changes of the internal (*Zang Fu*) organs and tissues.

1. *Yin symptom complexes*, a combination of signs related to interior, deficiency and cold: profuse sweating, shortness of breath, pallor, preference for hot drinks, cool skin, listlessness, pale moist tongue, weak pulse.

2. *Yang symptom complexes*, a combination of signs related to exterior, excess and hot: sticky sweating, rapid breathing, red face, preference for cold drinks, hot skin, restlessness, dry and red tongue, constipation, strong pulse.

Ying **(spring) points** [*Ying xue* 荥穴 *Vinh huyêt*], one of the **five transporting (*Shu*) points**, indicated in febrile disease (see **five transporting (*Shu*) points**).

Yuan **(source) points,** see **source (*Yuan*) points.**

Z

Zang Fu,   see **internal organs**.

Zang Fu **disharmony symptom complexes, diagnosis based on** [*Zang Fu bian zheng* 脏 腑 辨 证 *Tạng phủ biện chú'ng*],   one of the three methods of diagnosis. The two other methods are based on the eight guiding symptom complexes (*Ba gang bian zheng*) and on the symptom complexes of disharmony of the channels and collaterals (*Jing luo bian zheng*). When an organ is affected, the disorder may be restricted to that particular organ or it may influence or be influenced by disorders of other organs.

Zhang Ji (AD 150?-219?) [張 机 *Tru'o'ng Co'*],   a famous physician of the Han dynasty, author of several medical books, he is considered Hippocrates of the East. The most important of his books are *Treatise on Febrile and Miscellaneous Diseases* (*Shang han za bing lun*) and *Synopsis of Prescriptions of the Golden Chamber* (*Jin Kui yao lue fang lun*). He was the first to advocate the method of diagnosis based on the theory of six channels (*Liu jing bian zheng*) and on the eight guiding symptom complexes (*Ba gang bian zheng*). He was also considered the founder of the principle of treatment according to the method of differentiating symptoms and signs (*Bian zheng shi zhi*).

Zhang Jing-yue (about AD 1563-1640) [張 景 岳 *Tru'o'ng Cảnh Nhạc*],   author of several books on specified subjects such as pulse, paediatrics, gynaecology, surgery. His most important book is *The Systematic Compilation of the Internal Classic* (*Lei Jing*).

zone therapy,   see **reflexology**.

Appendices

Pinyin Phonetic Alphabet and Wade Giles System

WADE GILES SYSTEM		EXAMPLE
a	a	father
b	p	boy
c	ts', tz'	like 'ts' in its
ch	ch	chocolate
d	t	dog
e	e	her
f	f	for
g	k	get
h	h	house
i	i	machine
j	ch	joke
k	k'	cat
l	l	long
m	m	my
n	n	night
o	o	paw
p	p'	pass
q	ch'	like Ch in cheese
r	j	road or zenith
s	s, ss, sz	sad
sh	sh	shy
t	t'	tongue
u	u	moon or tu in French
v	v	used to pronounce foreign words
w	w	wash
x	hs	sheep

ACUPUNCTURE & MOXIBUSTION

	WADE GILES SYSTEM	EXAMPLE
y	y	young
z	ts, tz	zip
zh	ch	jump

Vowel combinations:

ai	like	ie	in	tie
ao	like	ow	in	owl
ei	like	ay	in	eight
ie	like	ie	in	deficient
ou	like	oe	in	toe

APPENDICES

Hanyupinyin Index

APPENDICES

ACUPUNCTURE & MOXIBUSTION

APPENDICES

Index of the 361 Regular Acupuncture Points

Dadu, Sp2	Big capital
Dadun, Liv1	Big plump
Dahe, K12	Great illustrious
Daheng, Sp15	Great transverse
Daju, St27	Exceedingly great
Daling, P7	Great mound
Daying, St5	Great greeting
Dazhong, K4	Big bell
Dazhu, UB11	Great shuttle
Dazhui, Gv14	Great vertebra
Daimai, GB26	Girdle channel
Danshu, UB19	Gall bladder *Shu*
Dicang, St4	Place granary
Diji, Sp8	Place crucial
Diwuhui, GB42	Place five reunions
Dushu, UB16	Governing vessel *Shu*
Dubi, St35	Calf nose
Duiduan, Gv27	Exchange extremity

E

Ermen, TH21	Ear gate
Erjian, LI2	Second opening

F

Feiyang, UB58	Flying up
Feishu, UB13	Lung *Shu*
Fenglong, St40	Great swell
Fenchi, GB20	Wind pond
Fengfu, Gv16	Wind palace
Fengmen, UB12	Wind door
Fengshi, GB31	Wind market
Fuyang, UB59	Instep *Yang*
Futu (Neck), LI18	Supporting rush
Fubai, GB10	Floating white
Fuxi, UB38	Floating cleft
Futu (Femur), St32	Hidden hare
Fushe, Sp13	Palace house
Fuliu, K7	Returning current
Fuai, Sp16	Abdomen grief
Fujie, Sp14	Abdomen node
Fufen, UB41	Supplementary division

APPENDICES

G

Ganshu, UB18 — Liver *Shu*
Gaohuangshu, UB43 — Vitals *Shu*
Geguan, UB46 — Diaphragm barrier
Geshu, UB17 — Diaphragm *Shu*
Gongsun, Sp4 — Grandfather grandson
Guanchong, TH1 — Barrier rushing
Guanmen, St22 — Closed door
Guanyuan, Cv4 — Barrier origin
Guanyuanshu, UB26 — Barrier origin *Shu*
Guangming, GB37 — Light bright
Guilai, St29 — Return arrive

H

Hanyan, GB4 — Jaw detested
Hegu, LI4 — Joining valley
Heyang, UB55 — Reunion *Yang*
Heliao (Ear), TH22 — Harmony bone
Heliao (Nose), LI19 — Grain bone
Henggu, K11 — Transverse bone, pubic bone
Houding, Gv19 — Posterior vertex
Houxi, SI3 — Back stream
Huaroumen, St24 — Smooth muscle door
Huagai, Cv20 — Splendid cover
Huantiao, GB30 — Circle jumping
Huangmen, UB51 — Vitals door
Huangshu, K16 — Vitals *Shu*
Huiyang, UB35 — Meeting of *Yang*
Huiyin, Cv1 — Meeting of *Yin*
Huizong, TH7 — Meeting origin
Hunmen, UB47 — Soul gate

J

Jimen, Sp11 — Basket door
Jiquan, H1 — Extreme spring
Jimai, Liv12 — Rapid pulse
Jizhong, Gv6 — Spine middle
Jiache, St6 — Jaw carriage, mandible
Jianjing, GB21 — Shoulder well
Jianliao, TH14 — Shoulder bone
Jianwaishu, SI14 — Shoulder outward *Shu*

Jianyu, LI15	Shoulder bone
Jianzhen, SI9	Shoulder upright
Jianzhongshu, SI15	Shoulder middle *Shu*
Jianshi, P5	Intermediary use
Jianli, Cv11	Built up mile
Jiaoxin, K8	Exchange news
Jiaosun, TH20	Horn grandson
Jiexi, St41	Enlarged stream
Jinmen, UB63	Golden gate
Jinsuo, Gv8	Contracted muscle
Jinggu, UB64	Great bone
Jingmen, GB25	Great gate
Jingming, UB1	Star bright
Jingqu, Lu8	Channel canal
Jiuwei, Cv15	Dove tail, xyphoid process
Juliao (Femur), GB29	Dwelling bone
Juliao (Nose), St3	Great bone
Jugu, LI16	Great bone
Juque, Cv14	Great watchtower
Jueyinshu, UB14	Absolute *Yin Shu*
Juegu (see *Xuanzhong*)	

K

Kongzui, Lu6	Supreme hole
Kufang, St14	Storehouse
Kunlun, UB60	Kunlun mountain

L

Laogong, P8	Labour palace
Ligou, Liv5	Woodworm ditch
Lidui, St45	Strict exchange
Lianquan, Cv23	Clean spring
Liangmen, St21	Beam door
Liangqiu, St34	Beam mound
Lieque, Lu7	Various openings
Lingdao, H4	Spirit path
Lingtai, Gv10	Sacred tower
Lingxu, K24	Spirit ruins
Lougu, Sp7	Leak valley
Luxi, TH19	Skull rest
Luoque, UB8	Connection deficiency

158

APPENDICES

M

Meichong, UB3 — Eyebrow rushing
Mingmen, Gv4 — Gate of life
Muchuang, GB16 — Eye window

N

Naohu, Gv17 — Brain house
Naokong, GB19 — Brain empty
Naohui, TH13 — Shoulder reunion
Naoshu, SI10 — Shoulder *Shu*
Neiguan, P6 — Inner barrier
Neiting, St44 — Inner courtyard

P

Pangguanshu, UB28 — Urinary bladder *Shu*
Pianli. LI6 — Spleen *Shu*
Pishu, UB20 — Deviated course
Pohu, UB42 — Inferior spirit shelter
Pushen, UB61 — Servant participating

Q

Qimen, Liv14 — Period gate
Qimai, TH18 — Clean vessel
Qichong, St30 — Rushing *Qi*
Qihai, Cv6 — Sea of *Qi*
Qihaishu, UB24 — Sea of *Qi Shu*
Qihu, St13 — *Qi* house
Qishe, St11 — *Qi* shelter
Qixue, K13 — *Qi* point
Qianding, Gv21 — Anterior vertex
Qiangu, SI2 — Anterior valley
Qianjian, Gv18 — Strong inbetween
Qingling, H2 — Green spirit
Qinglengyuan, TH11 — Limpid cold abyss
Qiuxu, GB40 — Mound ruins
Qubin, GB7 — Curved sideburns
Qucha, UB4 — Crooked uneven
Quchi, LI11 — Crooked pool
Qugu, Cv2 — Crooked bone, symphysis pubis
Ququan, Liv8 — Crooked spring
Quyuan, SI13 — Crooked wall

ACUPUNCTURE & MOXIBUSTION

Quze, P3 Crooked pond
Quanliao, SI18 Cheek bone
Quepen, St12 Notched basin

R
Rangu, K2 Burning valley
Renying, St9 Man greeting
Renzhong, Gv26 Man middle
Riyue, GB24 Sun moon
Rugen, St18 Breast root
Ruzhong, St17 Breast centre

S
Sanjian, LI3 Third opening
Sanjiaoshu, UB22 Three Heater *Shu*
Sanyangluo, TH8 Three *Yang* network
Sanyinjiao, Sp6 Three *Yin* meeting
Shanzhong, Cv17 Chest centre
Shangqiu, Sp5 Trade mound
Shangqu, K17 Shang tune
Shangyang, LI1 Trade *Yang*
Shangguan, GB3 Upper barrier
Shangjuxu, St37 Upper great void
Shanglian, LI9 Upper lateral aspect
Shangliao, UB31 Upper bone
Shangwan, Cv13 Upper gastric cavity
Shangxing, Gv23 Upper star
Shaochong, H9 Lesser rushing
Shaofu, H8 Lesser palace
Shaohai, H3 Lesser sea
Shaoshang, Lu11 Lesser trade
Shaoze, SI1 Lesser pond
Shenmai, UB62 Heavy vessel
Shenzhu, Gv12 Body pillar
Shencang, K25 Spirit shelter
Shendao, Gv11 Spirit path
Shenfeng, K23 Spirit seal
Shenmen, H7 Spirit door
Shenque, Cv8 Spirit watchtower
Shentang, UB44 Spirit hall
Shenting, Gv24 Spirit courtyard

APPENDICES

Shenshu, UB23	Kidney *Shu*
Shiguan, K18	Stone barrier
Shimen, Cv5	Stone gate
Shidou, Sp17	Food hole
Shousanli, LI10	Hand three miles
Shufu, K27	*Shu* palace
Shugu, UB65	Bound bone
Shuaigu, GB8	Guide valley
Shuidao, St28	Water way
Shuifen, Cv9	Water division
Shuiquan, K5	Water spring
Shuitu, St10	Water gushing
Sizhukong, TH23	Without silk bamboo
Sibai, St2	Four whites
Sidu, TH9	Four gutters
Siman, K14	Four fulls
Suliao, Gv25	Simple bone

T

Taibai, Sp3	Supreme white
Taichong, Liv3	Supreme rushing
Taixi, K3	Supreme spring
Taiyi, St23	Supreme *Yi*
Taiyuan, Lu9	Supreme abyss
Taodao, Gv13	Baking path
Tianchi, P1	Heavenly pond
Tianchong, GB9	Divine rushing
Tianchuang, SI16	Celestial window
Tianding, LI17	Heavenly urn
Tianfu, Lu3	Celestial palace
Tianjing, TH10	Celestial well
Tianliao, TH15	Heavenly bone
Tianquan, P2	Celestial spring
Tianrong, SI17	Divine appearance
Tianshu, St25	Heavenly pivot
Tiantu, Cv22	Divine charge
Tianxi, Sp18	Celestial stream
Tianyou, TH16	Heavenly window
Tianzhu, UB10	Heavenly pillar
Tianzhong, SI11	Divine origin
Tiaokou, St38	Regulating mouth

Tinggong, SI19	Hearing palace
Tinghui, GB2	Hearing meeting
Tonggu (Foot), UB66	Open valley
Tonggu (Abdomen), K20	Open valley
Tongli, H5	Inner communication
Tongtian, UB7	Leading to sky
Tongziliao, GB1	Pupil bone
Toulinqi, GB15	Head above star
Touqiaoyin, GB11	Head cavity *Yin*
Touwei, St8	Head tied

W

Waiguan, TH5	External barrier
Wailing, St26	External knoll
Waiqiu, GB36	Outer mound
Wangu (Head), GB12	Whole bone
Wangu (Hand), SI4	Wrist bone
Weidao, GB28	Binding path
Weiyang, UB39	Entrusting *Yang*
Weizhong, UB40	Entrusting middle
Weicang, UB50	Stomach granary
Weishu, UB21	Stomach *Shu*
Wenliu, LI7	Warm current
Wuyi, St15	House screen
Wuchu, UB5	Five areas
Wuli (Femur), Liv10	Five miles
Wuli (Hand), LI13	Five miles
Wushu, GB27	Five pivots

X

Xiguan, Liv7	Knee barrier
Xiyangguan, GB33	Knee *Yang* barrier
Ximen, P4	Gap door
Xiabai, Lu4	Chivalrous white
Xiaxi, GB43	Chivalrous stream
Xiaguan, St7	Lower barrier
Xiajuxu, St39	Lower great void
Xialian, LI8	Lower lateral aspect
Xialiao, UB34	Lower bone
Xiawan, Cv10	Lower stomach cavity
Xiangu, St43	Sunken valley

APPENDICES

Xiaoluo, TH12	Disappeared pleasure
Xiaochangshu, UB27	Small intestine *Shu*
Xiaohai, SI8	Small sea
Xinshu, UB15	Heart *Shu*
Xinhui, Gv22	Fontanelle reunion
Xingjian, Liv2	Go between
Xiongxiang, Sp19	Chest direction
Xuanji, Cv21	Rotary pearl
Xuanli, GB6	Suspended balance
Xuanlu, GB5	Suspended skull
Xuanshu, Gv5	Suspended pivot
Xuanzhong, GB39	Suspended bell
Xuehai, Sp10	Sea of blood
Y	
Yamen, Gv15	Mutism gate
Yangbai, GB14	*Yang* white
Yangchi, TH4	*Yang* pond
Yangfu, GB38	*Yang* support
Yanggang, UB48	*Yang* fundamental
Yanggu, SI5	*Yang* valley
Yangjiao, GB35	*Yang* crossing
Yanglingquan, GB34	*Yang* knoll spring
Yangxi, LI5	*Yang* stream
Yanglao, SI6	Nursing the elderly
Yaoshu, Gv2	Lumbar *Shu*
Yaoyangguan, Gv3	Lumbar *Yang* barrier
Yemen, TH2	Fluid gate
Yishe, UB49	Thought shelter
Yixi, UB45	Happy idea
Yifeng, TH17	Windscreen
Yinmen, UB37	Rich gate
Yinbao, Liv9	*Yin* envelope
Yindu, K19	*Yin* capital
Yingu, K10	*Yin* valley
Yinjiao (Abdomen), Cv7	*Yin* crossing
Yinlian, Liv11	*Yin* lateral aspect
Yinlingquan, Sp9	*Yin* knoll spring
Yinshi, St33	*Yin* market
Yinxi, H6	*Yin* gap
Yinjiao (Mouth), Gv28	Gums crossing

ACUPUNCTURE & MOXIBUSTION

Yinbai, Sp1 — Hidden white
Yingchuan, St16 — Chest window
Yingxiang, LI20 — Greeting fragrance
Yongquan, K1 — Gushing spring
Youmen, K21 — Obscure gate, pylorus
Yuji, Lu10 — Fish border
Yutang, Cv18 — Jade hall
Yuzhen, UB9 — Jade pillow
Yuzhong, K26 — Stagnant middle
Yuanye, GB22 — Armpit abyss
Yunmen, Lu2 — Cloud door

Z

Zanzhu, UB2 — Gathering bamboo
Zhangmen, Liv13 — Chapter gate
Zhaohai, K6 — Shining sea
Zhejin, GB23 — Adjoining muscle
Zhengying, GB17 — Main enterprise
Zhigou, TH6 — Collateral drain
Zhizhong, SI7 — Main branch
Zhishi, UB52 — Will house
Zhiyang, Gv9 — Reaching *Yang*
Zhiyin, UB67 — Reaching *Yin*
Zhibian, UB54 — Order edge
Zhongchong, P9 — Middle rushing
Zhongdu (Foot), Liv6 — Central capital
Zhongdu (Femur), GB32 — Middle of ditch
Zhongfen, Liv4 — Middle sealing
Zhongfu, Lu1 — Central palace
Zhongji, Cv3 — Between poles
Zhongliao, UB33 — Middle bone
Zhonglushu, UB29 — Middle spine *Shu*
Zhongshu, Gv7 — Central pivot
Zhongting, Cv16 — Central courtyard
Zhongwan, Cv12 — Middle of gastric cavity
Zhongzhu (Hand), TH3 — Middle islet
Zhongzhu (Abdomen), K15 — Middle pouring
Zhourong, Sp20 — All around flourishing
Zhouliao, LI12 — Elbow bone
Zhubin, K9 — Construction bank
Zigong (Chest), Cv19 — Purple palace

APPENDICES

Zulingqi, GB41	Foot above tears
Zuqiaoyin, GB44	Foot *Yin* cavity
Zusanli, St36	Leg three miles

APPENDICES

Chinese Weights and Measures

	CHINESE SYSTEM	METRIC SYSTEM	GB & US SYSTEM
Length	*Fen* *Cun*: 10 *Fen* *Chi*: 10 *Cun* *Zhang*: 10 *Chi* *Li*: 150 *Zhang*	0.33cm 3.33cm 0.33m 3.33m 500m	1.31 in 1.09 ft 3.64 yd 0.31 mile
Area	*Pingfang Chi* *Pingfang Zhang* *Pingfang Li* *Mu*: 60 *Pingfang* *Zhang*	$0.11m^2$ $11.11m^2$ $0.25km^2$ 0.06 ha	1.19 sq ft 13.28 sq yd 0.09 sq mile 0.16 acre
Capacity	*He* *Sheng* *Dou* *Shi*	1 dl 1 l 10 l 100 l	0.17 pt 0.22 gal 2.19 gal 2.74 bu
Weight	*Qian* *Liang*: 10 *Qian* *Jin*: 10 *Liang* *Dan*: 100 *Chin*	5g 50g 500g 50kg	0.17 oz 1.76 oz 1.10 lb 110.23 lb

Synopsis of Chinese Medical History

ACUPUNCTURE & MOXIBUSTION

YEARS	DYNASTIES		EVENTS
4480-4365 BC 3220-3080 2700-2600 2359-2259 2256-2208	Fu Hshi Shen Nong Huang Di Yao Sun		Use of stone, bone, bamboo needles to cure diseases in primitive society. Legendary period, the age of the Five Emperors.
2205-1766 1176-1122	Hsia Shang		Earliest record of traditional Chinese medicine in the beginning of the Shang dynasty.
1122-250	Chou	Eastern Chou 770-256	Bian Que, earliest famous physician (about 500 BC). Huang Di's *Internal Classic (Nei Jing)*.
		Spring-Autumn 770-476	Early medical organizations with four kinds of physicians in charge of Nutrition, Internal medicine, Surgery, Veterinary.
		Warring-States 475-221	Earliest case history recording system. Annual professional assessment of physicians to determine salary and grade.
221-207	Qin		Development and success of empirical medicine from the Qin dynasty to the Ming dynasty.

APPENDICES

YEARS	DYNASTIES		EVENTS
206 BC–AD 220	Han	Western Han (Former Han) 206 BC–AD 24	Hua Tuo (AD 141-212), father of anaesthesia and surgery. *Historical Records* by Szuma Chien (145-90 BC).
		Eastern Han (Later Han)	*Treatise on Fever and Miscellaneous Diseases and Synopsis of Prescriptions of the Golden Chamber* by Zhang Ji (AD 150?-219). *Difficult Classic (Nan Jing)*.
220-280	Three Kingdoms	Wei Shu Wu	
265-420	Jin		*A Classic of Acupuncture and Moxibustion* by Huangfu Mi (AD 214-282), earliest book on acupuncture and moxibustion. *Classic of the Pulse* by Wang Xi (AD 210-285).
420-589	Northern Dynasties Southern Dynasties		*Collection on Commentaries on the Pharmacopoeia Classic* by Taohong Jing (AD 452-536).
581-618	Sui		Foundation of the Imperial Medical College with acupuncture and moxibustion as a definite unit in the medical department.

ACUPUNCTURE & MOXIBUSTION

YEARS	DYNASTIES	EVENTS
618-907	Tang	Establishment of the Imperial Academy of Medicine with four departments: internal medicine, acupuncture, massage, sorcery.
		Prescriptions Worth a Thousand Gold and *Supplement to Prescriptions Worth a Thousand Gold* by Sun Si-miao (AD 581-682).
907-960	Five Dynasties	Development and progress in acupuncture and moxibustion.
960-1279	Song	Foundation of the Imperial Medical Bureau with nine departments including the department of acupuncture and moxibustion.
		Illustrated Manual on the Points for Acupuncture and Moxibustion as found on the bronze figure published in AD 1207 by Wang Wei-yi (about AD 987-1067).
		Casting of two life-size hollow bronze figures on the surface of which were located all the points through which water can flow out, used for teaching and testing the candidates.
		Foundation of an official agency to supply and dispense herbal medicines.
		Revision and publication of ancient medical literature thanks to the development of the printing.

YEARS	DYNASTIES	EVENTS
916-1125	Liao	Graphic illustrations of thirty-six varieties of pulse prepared by Xu Shu-wei (AD 1079-1154?).
1115-1234	Jin	School of Cold and Cold Medicine founded by Liu Wan-su (about AD 1120-1200), author of *The Aetiology Based on Su Wen*.
		School for Nourishing the Earth or Strengthening the Stomach founded by Li Gao (AD 1180-1251), author of the *Treatise on the Spleen and the Stomach*.
		Attacking and Purgative School founded by Zhang Congzheng (about AD 1156-1228).
1271-1368	Yuan	Zhu Zhen-heng (AD 1280-1358) founded the School for Nourishing the *Yin*.
		Hua Shou (AD 1304-1386), author of *The Expounding of the Fourteen Channels*, recomposed the *Difficult Classic* (*Nan Jing*).

ACUPUNCTURE & MOXIBUSTION

YEARS	DYNASTIES	EVENTS
1368-1644	Ming	Big progress in medicine and pharmacology. Foundation of the Royal College of Medicine. *Compendium of Materia Medica* and *The Pulse Study of Bin Hu* by Li Shi-zhen (AD 1518-1593). *Compendium of Acupuncture and Moxibustion* by Yang Ji-zhou (AD 1522-1620). *Catechism of Acupuncture and Moxibustion* by Wang Ji (AD 1463-1539).
1644-1911	Qing	Publication of a large number of medical books, among them several books on cold-induced diseases. From the middle of the dynasty, decline and finally ban on acupuncture and moxibustion from the Imperial Medical College curriculum in 1822. In total, more than 3000 medical titles have been published from the Han to the end of the Qing dynasty.
1911-1949	Republic of China	Traditional Chinese medicine prohibited in 1929.

APPENDICES

YEARS	DYNASTIES	EVENTS
1949-	People's Republic of China	Renaissance of the traditional Chinese medicine, acupuncture and moxibustion. Effort to integrate traditional Chinese medicine in Western medicine. Development of new methods of acupuncture such as acupuncture analgesia, scalp acupuncture, electro-acupuncture etc.

References

Beijing Foreign Languages Press (1981)
Essentials of Chinese Acupuncture.
Fu Wei-kang (1975)
The Story of Chinese Acupuncture and Moxibustion.
Foreign Languages Press, Beijing.
Huard, P. and Wong, Ming (1968)
Chinese Medicine.
World University Library, McGraw-Hill, New York.
Kaptchuk, Ted J. (1983)
Chinese Medicine: The Web That Has No Weaver.
Rider & Company, Hutchinson Publishing Group, London.
Liu, F. and Liu, Y.M. (1980)
Chinese Medical Terminology.
The Commercial Press Ltd., Hong Kong.
Mann, F.
— *Acupuncture: The Ancient Chinese Art of Healing* (1978)
— *The Treatment of Diseases by Acupuncture* (1973)
W. Heinemann Medical Books Ltd., London.
Medicine & Health Publishing Co., Hong Kong (1973)
*An Explanatory Book of the Newest Illustrations of Acupuncture
Points.*
Omura, Y. (1982)
Acupuncture Medicine: Its Historical and Clinical Backgrounds.
Japan Publishing Inc., Tokyo.
Ou Ming, et al. (1982)
*Chinese-English Glossary of Common Terms in Traditional Chinese
Medicine.*
Joint Publishing Co., Hong Kong.
People's Medical Publishing House, Beijing.
— *A Concise Chinese English Dictionary of Medicine* (1982).
— *English-Chinese Glossary of Basic Medical Terms* (1976).

ACUPUNCTURE & MOXIBUSTION

Shandong Sciences & Technology Press. (1982)
  Anatomical Atlas of Chinese Acupuncture Points.
Shanghai College of Traditional Medicine.
  Acupuncture: A Comprehensive Text. (1981)
  Translated and edited by John O'Connor and Dan Bensky, Eastland
  Press.
Soulié de Morant, G. (1972)
  Acupuncture chinoise.
  Maloine, Paris.
Veith Ilza. (1972)
  The Yellow Emperor's Classic of Internal Medicine.
  University of California Press.
Wallnofer, H. and Anna V. Rottauscher. (1975)
  Chinese Folk Medicine and Acupuncture.
  White Lion Publishers Ltd., London.